**The Body:** the [...] ith its own distinct functio[...] onality. It is the "you" othe[...] comfortably familiar and maddeningly inscrutable to the [...] inhabits it—at once a vessel, a dear friend, a stern judge, and a treacherous betrayer.

In *Body,* eighteen great contemporary American writers explore the singular components of this extraordinary whole, in short literary observations and appreciations that range from the visceral to the whimsical to the sinful and metaphysical. In "Eyes," Michael Knight explores the biological evolution of sight and unexpectedly discovers a hidden truth about human love. Leah Hager Cohen examines the dichotomies of "Breasts"—a source of life . . . or poison. Jacki Lyden considers the thought processes and questionable memories of her mother—and their funny and heartbreaking familial repercussions—in "The Brain." Richard McCann offers a powerful, startling, and darkly humorous personal look at organ transplantation in "The Resurrectionist." And Pulitzer Prize winner Jane Smiley's riveting "Belly, Dancing, Belly, Aching, Belly, Beasts" celebrates the female abdomen in its many incarnations: swollen and distended with life; flat with sexuality; ripened with age.

A strong and worthy literary companion to the critically acclaimed anthologies *Family* and *Home, Body* is, by turns, passionate and serene, sensuous, urgent, tender, and tragic—illuminated by dazzling wit and incandescent beauty—and it will enthrall anyone and everyone who lives and breathes and delights in the written word.

"The body of this anthology is not always sexy, or even pleasant to look at. Rather, with its scars, pounding hearts, and torn cuticles, it is the always aging container of our lived experiences. . . . This formula works because of the range of writing and insights invited, even when the experience of reading it produces the pleasure of a well-turned phrase rather than the revelation of a startling insight. . . . For anyone who likes reading essays, these have real body."

—*Philadelphia City Paper*

# BODY

# BODY

edited *by* Sharon Sloan Fiffer

*and* Steve Fiffer

Perennial

*An Imprint of* HarperCollins*Publishers*

"Breasts" by Leah Hager Cohen originally appeared in *Self.*
"The Resurrectionist" by Richard McCann originally appeared in *Tin Roof.*
"A Note on the Dink" by Ron Carlson originally appeared in *Esquire.*
"The Blessings of the Butt" originally appeared in *Salon.*
"Hair" by Veronica Chambers originally appeared in the June 1999
issue of *Vogue.*

A hardcover edition of this book was published by Bard, an imprint
of Avon Books, Inc., in 1999.

HarperCollins books may be purchased for educational, business, or sales
promotional use. For information please write: Special Markets Department,
HarperCollins Publishers Inc., 10 East 53rd Street, New York, NY 10022.

First Perennial edition published 2000.

*Designed by Kellan Peck*

The Library of Congress has catalogued the hardcover edition as follows:
Body / edited by Sharon Sloan Fiffer and Steve Fiffer.—1st ed.
p. cm.
"An Avon book."
1. Authors, American—20th century—Biography. 2. Body, Human—
Psychological aspects. I. Fiffer, Sharon Sloan, 1951– . II. Fiffer, Steve.
PS135.B63 1999                                                    99-21618
814'.5408035—dc21                                                      CIP

ISBN 0-380-80358-5 (pbk.)

00 01 02 03 04 ❖/RRD 10 9 8 7 6 5 4 3 2 1

*To Kate, Nora, and Rob—our favorite bodies of work.*

Love's mysteries in souls do grow
But yet the body is his book.

—JOHN DONNE

# CONTENTS

# INTRODUCTION

It may be our minds that govern us, our souls that guide us, but it is our bodies on which our histories are written, in which our stories are embedded. Here, in *Body,* eighteen writers expose themselves in the most literary, if not literal, sense. Painful, honest, thoughtful, witty, and arresting, each essay presents one writer's exploration of one part of his or her body.

When we, as editors, invite such a talented and eclectic group of writers to the table, or in this case a better metaphor might be the examining table, we, along with every reader of this book, are likely to have some expectations. We all have bodies, we know what they do, how they function, how they provide pleasure, give pain, resist, yield, succeed, and fail. But it is in the particulars of the feet, the hands, the belly, the knee, the skin, and the scars where we grow fascinated. Through the eyes and ears of others we rethink our visions of self. Our own flesh and blood meditations grow from the questions posed by the womb, the breast, and the ownership and receivership of the liver. We rethink the way men and women define themselves through the visible—hair and teeth—and the not-so-visible physicality of sex. It is with brain and heart we reason and feel, we consider and reconsider the body.

The religious philosopher Teilhard de Chardin once suggested we rethink our place in the world. Instead of regarding ourselves as human beings struggling to have some kind of spiritual experience, perhaps, he mused, we should consider the possibility that we are spiritual beings having a human experience. And the human experience, as we know, for better or worse, is lived in the body.

This collection of personal essays is warm, alive, and ticking with a powerful pulse. Enjoy its energy and revelations. Aspire to the life of the mind if you will, but right now, welcome to the life of the *Body*.

# BODY

# MICHAEL KNIGHT

> To suppose that the eye, with all its inimitable contrivances for
> adjusting the focus to different distances, for admitting different
> amounts of light, and for the correction of spherical and chromatic
> aberration, could have been formed by natural selections, seems, I
> freely confess, absurd in the highest possible degree.
> —Charles Darwin

Darwin himself worried that the human eye would be the
spoiler of evolutionary theory. Seventeen major parts in the standard textbook diagram—cornea, iris, assorted nerves, et cetera—
each one integral to the working of the others. And, so far,
science has yet to produce a definitive explanation for the way
in which these components have come to develop. One day
blind amoeba danced in a prehistoric soup, some hundred million days later, give or take, they knew light and varieties of
dark, they knew the dazzle of color, they knew what it was to
lie on the ground and watch galaxies spinning in the sky. There
is nothing gradual in the case of the eye, the way I understand
it, no fins morphing into legs, no gills snake-charming into
lungs. There is no straight line between blindness and sight.

Witness my wife: Each morning she stands before the mirror in our bedroom preparing herself for work. She believes that I am still visionless with sleep, believes that she will wake me in a few minutes and we will adjourn to the kitchen for a cup of coffee before we say good-bye. But I am not asleep at all. I can see everything. Her elegant legs and bare shoulders flushed from the shower. Her fragile neck made pale by a recent haircut. Her hands flicking from a makeup kit atop the dresser to her face. Her eyes peer mysteriously into themselves. She has blue eyes, my wife, flecked with green and gold. I want to say, My eyes are a secret, as are yours, beyond methodology and science. Even now, I cloak them in lowered lashes and pretend that I am dreaming.

The eyes can't be trusted. The ciliary muscle, for instance, is a band of tissue with no other purpose than to regulate the flattening and hardening of the lens. The lens, in turn, throws light on the retina, the retina contains the rods and cones and is connected to the optic nerve and so on, and, like a network of spies, not one of them can be explained except in terms of its compatriots. Demand evolution from your vitreous humor and it dissolves into gelatinous ooze. More than that, eyes are full of pranks and distortions, half-truths and outright lies. A woman in Mississippi glimpses Christ in the condensation on a convenience store refrigerator. A man in the desert spots shimmering trees and cool water where there is only sand. My wife wakes screaming in the middle of the night because the lovers in a painting have stepped out of the canvas and are standing beside our bed. Much to my surprise, as I jar awake and reach across to comfort her, I see what she is seeing—their arms linked in the half-light, matching pairs of pupil-less eyes—and I can't help but scream with her. I ditch the covers and paw the air. My wife gets a lamp going and we blink away our fear. Later, when she is asleep with her head on my chest, I remember how she looked in the nightmareless light, her eyes aglow with worry—her eyes, her eyes—pillow lines drawn like filigree on her cheeks.

The first time I really looked at my wife, slowed down and let my gaze linger a while, she was drinking from a water fountain, bent at the waist, water playing against her lips. She wore a suede jacket, I recall, and a white turtleneck and blue jeans. Her shoes were brown leather. Her hair was pushed behind her ear. I had seen her before, passed her in hallways and on sidewalks, spoken to her in class, but this time, as my eyes broke her into light and recast her as herself, she cocked her head and smiled, still drinking, her own eyes crinkling at the corners. She curled her fingers at me and wiped her mouth with the back of her hand. That was no lie. She swears, these days, that she wasn't interested in me then. She was just being friendly, she says, she hardly remembers the day at all. But I was there, my heart racing, my brain wiped clean of conversation. I know what I saw.

Now and then, my wife jokes that she would like me to gaze more amorously into her eyes—in the practiced manner of romantic leads on television—before kissing her. But whenever I try it, whenever I make a conscious effort to summon all the things that I am feeling and project those feelings through my pupils, both of us dissolve with laughter over how ridiculous I look. My eyes bulge with love. Nose to nose, my eyes go crooked with desire.

Simply put, the eye works like a camera. Light enters the pupil, is focused by the lens which forms an inverted image on the retina. No fossils bear prehistoric examples of the human eye, something rudimentary and flawed like the smoking box cameras in old Westerns. Variations of eyes are manifest in different species, of course: The bumblebee's faceted eyes, like peering through diamonds, or the dog who sees the world in degrees of black and white. Primitive amoeba possessed patches of photosensitive cells, but sensitivity to light is not the same as seeing any more than knowing the sun is in the sky is the same as witnessing light streaming down through the branches of the trees. Tracking an evolutionary path for the eye is akin to leaping zigzag across a river from stone to distant stone. All of which are part of the reason, I suppose, that the eye has maintained its metaphorical power for such a long time. The eye is baffling and elusive, the last line of defense for hard-core creationists and the first place my wife looks to know what's happening in my head and heart.

My wife and I play chess now and then on the coffee table in the living room, TV flicking mutely by the sliding door. I showed her how to play the game during our first year of dating and within a week she was beating me sometimes. She is an aggressive player, my wife. When she looks at the board, she sees various avenues of attack, whereas I see nothing but pitfalls. I hang back and wait for her to give me an opening. Her eyes intent, a finger playing back and forth across her lips. She is tenacious in our marriage, too. She loves like a fistfight, a blur of contact and emotion. She believes, with the certainty of a thousand poets, in the expressive power of the human eye. When she is angry, she searches my eyes for signs of contrition. When she is most in love, she scans my pupils for reciprocation as though there is some undiagrammed pipeline between my eyes and my heart. I want her to understand that my eyes are devious, overcautious little sneaks. Look at them now, stealing glimpses across a chessboard, running the length of her forearm, settling craftily on her lips, her brow, a bike-wreck scar on the bridge of her nose, then glancing away like schoolboys when she looks up from her move.

Regarding eyes, most scientists recommend context and restraint. There has been life on earth of one kind or another for millions of years, they say. It may seem unlikely that such a complicated piece of machinery as the eye could be derived from the membrane of a single-celled organism and the evidence, for the moment, may be partly theoretical but the evolution of the eye, they say, is less impossible than God. What it boils down to plainly is a question of belief. Where and with whom do you want to put your faith? When I was a boy, maybe nine or ten, I was convinced beyond a doubt that ghosts were real. I gave a speech on the afterlife in class, cited all sorts of dubious testimony, conveniently ignored documentation to the contrary. I stacked the deck in favor of my belief. But I'm still not wholly convinced that I was wrong. Faith dies hard and, sometimes, if you're lucky, it doesn't die at all. Now, nearly twenty years later, I want to believe that it is possible for a man to see a woman drinking from a water fountain and love her for the rest of his life. That such a fragile, intricate, perhaps miraculous, organ as the eye, all full of wiles and inconsistencies, has delivered unto me one indisputable truth: There is a woman drinking from a water fountain. Simple, no mirage, no tricks of light. There is the water and there are her lips. How could I not believe in her?

My wife and I have been married just over four months as this is being written, though we have been together most of four years. We live in a rental cottage on someone else's farm and in the evening we sit on the porch and play cards or chess and rehash our respective days. We can see mountains from our house and cattle and fireflies, none of which serves as proof of everlasting love. The enormity, the sheer weight of the promise we made to each other still strikes me sometimes, makes my hands shake and takes my breath away. Such a guarantee is as absurd as religion, as preposterous as evolution. I read somewhere that Darwin's wife, Emma, made doubtful margin notes in her husband's essay on natural selection because of the problems presented by the eye. Imagine the leap of faith she was called upon to make. I think of my own wife, inside now, talking to her mother on the phone, and I wonder how difficult it was for her to trust herself to someone like me, someone whose feelings are more quiet than she would like, someone who has a hard time shining love through ineloquent pupils. Then she turns the corner into my line of sight and my eyes work their magic, reversing her on my retinas, rods and cones sorting out the quality of light, which in this case is evening light, delicate and golden and edged with shadow. I can see her hands and pale skin and the way fabric moves against her legs. I can see her own eyes, usually so bold, going shy when she notices that I'm watching.

# THE BRAIN

---

## JACKI LYDEN

My mother believes she is a Mafioso's daughter. In her brain, she is the daughter of Frank Balistrieri, leader of the Milwaukee underworld in the 1970s. "A chief without any Indians," the feds tell me, and so they had to bring him down in the end using outside help. They recruited one of their own double agents from New York—an FBI agent who had infiltrated the Bonanno family. He came out and strong-armed Frank and told him the Bonannos wanted in on Frank's vending machine operation. The whole thing was phony anyway, and that's how the feds nailed Mr. Balistrieri from their listening post. I love it that my mother's "godfather" went to prison through subterfuge and an assumed identity. For in her delusions, my mother often changes her name and identity, as well. The undercover agent the feds called in from New York was awesome they said, just like the real thing, a guy called Joe Pistone. The Bonannos knew him as someone else—Donnie Brasco. Donnie Brasco . . . Johnny Depp played him in the movie of the same name. Maybe you saw it.

That's how it is with my mother's brain. I pull a thread and I wind up with Johnny Depp, or Donnie Brasco, or Frank

Balistrieri, a big hood in his own half-imaginary Sicilian soap opera. A man who died fifteen years ago, shortly after his release from prison, a man whom it can be justly said never did anybody any good and is wholly gone now. Except in my mother's brain, which has been turned into a lounge show, or underworld red velvet Mafia joint, in which he lolls about throwing lit cigarettes and demanding respect and her lifetime allegiance. It's ironic, really, that in a way this dead man gets from my mother what he could not acquire in the bad old times. Frank Balistrieri, like a mad scientist, has stolen my mother's brain. Though you could also say she gave it to him.

Balistrieri is Armageddon in my mother's brain. He is the destroyer, and then the creator of life, so pervasive that he has become the unseen presence shaping her life's loops and cul de sacs—her secret parentage, of course; her marriages, her commitments on and off for thirty years to mental wards. Even now, she sees his hand writ large in her affairs. "People keep an eye on me, Jacki," she'll say. "My car is bugged, but it's for a reason. My godfather wants to protect me." Occasionally, she will tell me she is planning to change her name to reflect her true identity, and I warn her that she has done this too often, and that I will tip off the FBI if she dares to try. I will say anything to keep her in line, but confess I am somewhat disappointed. Shouldn't I be the architect of her brain, if she is going to allow dominance by someone other than herself? After all, I have written about her brain, documented it, done battle with it for all these years. I am her oldest child and confidant. When she left the hospital for what I hoped would be the final time, her brain had been treated by a new alchemy. I believed that the delusions amid which she drifted and rode would recede into the caverns from whence they had come. And so they largely have. We chop up her lithium pills on the sideboard along with the celery and the carrots, as if the pills were seeds used to provide the flavor of reality.

Except I cannot chop up this damn Balistrieri. He represents, I think, my mother's manic attraction to power, to the means to create and to extinguish life, to the fount of the delusions of grandeur. That is a phrase now drained of potency for me, suitable for posting over a Las Vegas wedding chapel. Potent Frank Balistrieri is a man whom lithium fails to knock out. He has always remained, the brain's uninvited guest, squiring her around and taking credit for loads of things he scarcely deserves—"Some men came into the office. I think they were just there to check up on me. One of them laid a sawed-off shotgun on my desk. After that, I got the bonus check to buy a new car!" To Balistrieri goes the wholly unwarranted credit, and I take it personally. I try to snub him, hoping that by suppressing all her conversation about his accomplishments he will have neither voice nor entrée into my mother's larger interaction with the world. Snub him? I garrote him, pour acid in his eyes, knife his heart. It's hopeless, impossible to do battle with a shadow. The truth is that some of the brain's tints and poses are over time its own indelible work of art. Balistrieri is figured in my mother's mind, carved and patterned there like the paintings in the Lascaux caves. Her secret father arms her with invincible powers, sets her step before the world.

Balistrieri, a man deceased, is in my mother's brain merely terminally ill. He has been terminally ill for over a decade now and I am beginning to imagine him like Vincent Price in his coffin, getting up but only for grand entrances. No wonder, I hiss to myself, she can't *find* him, he's *dead*. But not to her, for there are heirs. I learned only very recently that a decade or so ago my mother sought out Balistrieri's son. It turned out the poor man did a little time with his father in prison as well, but this man is today a jovial hotelier in a city I won't name. He has a boulevardier's personality by the sound of it. When I question him on the telephone he says, "Wow. You know, I think I met your mother. Little woman? Dark hair? Yes, she came to my office eight or nine years ago. Very attractive. She said she was my half-sister. What a story! I almost believed her, y'know, because my father—well, I won't get into that but you wanna talk about crazy! We went through all the dates and I just had to tell her they didn't add up, y'know. Say, it's really nice to talk to you!" I learned a few other things about his life. That he lives alone. On the weekends, he said, it's a "party of three . . . me, the couch and the radio." I feel a family kinship with him. Obviously, he is not enjoying being Balistrieri's son nearly as much as my mother is enjoying being his daughter. "The stories I could tell you," he sighs.

I sigh back. I vow never to tell my mother of junior B's conversation. She has shown me "the Don's" cuff links and told me how he loved her as a daughter, how she keeps his memory alive by lighting candles. One of these days, she says, she is going to write her own book. Sure, I say, you just go right ahead. I imagine a strenuously purple tome. A year or so ago, she started telling guests at my sister's dinner gathering all about her Mafia father. "He knows everything I do," she said. "He's having me watched." I have told her not to speak of the Don if possible. Listen, I say, don't you know that under the strict codes of *omerta* you are obligated to silence? I know, Jacki, she says, what do you think I am, stupid? Of course I want her to keep silent, but only because I want her to show the world that she is a smashing testimony to overcoming mental illness. And except for that damn Balistrieri, she is. When we go on the Oprah Winfrey show, I am sandwiched between my mother and Oprah on national television. The effect is to say the least profoundly disorienting. My mother is much more composed than I who live in the afterglow of her life's delusions. Listen, I have instructed my mother—don't you dare bring him up on *Oprah*. Don't you say a word. Do you think I'm some kind of idiot? she replies.

"So," says Oprah, an icon like the Delphic oracle, "what does a nervous breakdown feel like?" She is dressed in flowing red garments, glowing monitors her sacred fires and the chorus, of course, all about us. "Feel" is a long drawn-out word.

I hold my breath. My mother's voice is steady.

"Confusion," says my mother, and the audience murmurs approval. "But I think I was always confused about my identity." My stomach tightens. My mother looks serious.

Oprah smiles and moves on, and once again, the searchlights have missed that Sicilian figure skulking under the walls of the labyrinth.

The truth is that compared to the other uninvited guests in my mother's brain over past years, the powerful Mafioso is a sufficiently benign presence. He's more or less a big pussycat rather than a blood-drenched henchman. But I do mind the way he has vanquished my grandmother and her husband. Last

Christmas in Wisconsin, when I arrived home on Christmas Eve my mother had on a bright green blazer, quilted red vest and ruffly white blouse. She wore a brooch of small bells that had belonged to my grandmother—or as my mother refers now to that ragged-voiced denizen of her imagination, "Mabel, the woman who took care of me." The bells on Mabel's brooch jingle as my mother spins a green, red and white blur before my eyes.

"Hi there!" I say, half-dead. My plane has grounded in Chicago and I've driven with total strangers to Wisconsin. Everyone's waiting. "Look at those colors," I say, amused. "The Christmas elf!"

"These aren't Christmas colors," my mother protests. "These are the colors of the Italian flag!" Later I examine the cookbook next to the table. Under the recipe for Mexican chili, my mother has crossed out *Mexican* and written *Italian*. We have an all-Italian meal. Everything we eat is either red or white or green—lime Jell-O, mashed potatoes, rich tomato chili. An edible fantasy and presiding over the table—I must beg your indulgence to believe me—my mother, who with the sculpting of a beautiful age has indeed come to look Sicilian. In a life buoyed and resonant with her secrets, her high cheekbones and dark eyes and hair are clear and sharp. The night is a confection warmed up in Italy.

And the more my brain unwillingly complies with this altered reality, the more the voice of my grandmother caterwauls in the recesses of the bungalow where my mother lives. The bungalow once belonged to my grandmother, Mabel, but has been renovated to a chicness that would baffle the old fishwife.

We sit at the Christmas table, and my grandmother's words bawl at the back of my brain. "She dassn't think I'm good enough for her. You wanna beer? Here's my Frederick's of Hollywood book, would you hide it under the bed for me? Wouldja bring me my cigs? Get the fan, we'll blow the smoke outside and hide it from your ma. You wanna ice cream? I could take you to the drive-in. I got muskrat soup. You don't like it, I got turtle. Fresh-caught." My mother interrupts my reverie and raises a glass of eggnog. "Here's to poor old Mabel," she says. "She had no choice but to take me in. They needed the money and there were threats. She had to hide me in that awful alley basement apartment, of course. Anyway, someday I will tell about the cover-up."

I have never been able to figure out my mother's disdain for her mother, when Mabel would cheerfully have walked on hot coals for her daughter. It is true that Mabel was uncouth and foulmouthed where my mother had pretensions to much better, but then, we all have our failings, and Mabel's floury hands, rockety gray hair and green-glass eyeshades call out to me much more lustily than Balistrieri's gangsterism. My mother cannot hear her mother's voice any longer, but my sister, who has inherited some of my mother's alchemy, claims she can hear it and more.

"I saw her, Jack," she says. "She was sitting right out here on the porch. I could see the condensation on the porch windows, the deer leg with its thermometer. 'Mabes,' I says, 'do you come here often?' 'No', she says, 'this is a kind of a meeting place'. 'You must be happy', I says, 'with all your brothers and sisters and your husband Ray in heaven.' 'Oh, I am,' she says, 'I am.' "

I blink. From my sister Kate's account, Mabel seems happier in the afterlife and more at rest than the constantly strutting Frank Balistrieri, who seems to have a lot of unfinished business on earth. My mother keeps him busy, I guess, as her protector.

She's so good at the delusion of being Frank Balistrieri's daughter that I am beginning to live in that Sicilian borogove her brain has sown. I have a notebook. It's a family tree drawn by my mother in one of her more manic eras. An elaborate vine twists over manila pages, like frost on a pane, and at the head of the snaking leaves is Balistrieri's name. The story she writes spells out the tale of Balistrieri's secret liaison with Mabel's sister Martha, her "real" mother.

*If this had been known in 1930 it would have shocked society!!!!* it says, in a big, hyperventilating and yet girlish hand.

She has cooked up for Martha a kind of glamorous café society profile, though I believe Martha tied flies in a sporting goods factory up north for a living. Somehow though, mysteriously, she did get a little money. Hence my mother's affinity. Pasted in the book my mother has included a photo of herself on a pony ride, age about ten, and she has changed her name beneath the photo to Balistrieri. She writes that she is the daughter of *Shame and Confusion*. And as I turn the pages, there are the pictures of these incarnations, her real parents, Ray and Mabel, holding my mother as a baby between them. They are wearing old-fashioned swimsuits, and Ray peers down adoringly, muscles as hard as the dock loader he in fact is. My mother has reconfigured history, redesigned it with a romantic, Sicilian twist. Her creation is the brain's work of art.

My mother never stops to think, cannot stop to think, that if she were truly a Mafioso's daughter then I would be a Mafioso's granddaughter. That would cancel out my grandfather, a man I never knew. The brawny fighter, Ray, who at age fifty believed he could deter a barroom bandit. A fatal bullet became his final benediction. Like my mother, he must have believed in the principle of invincibility. This belief is as mysterious to me as any gift of inspiration. My grandfather's brain must have borne a picture of himself as a man who could stop time. And his death did in fact cleave time for my mother, dividing her life through the decades, until Frank Balistrieri mossed over that memory too, pushing up through the barroom floorboards where my grandfather used to lay. It all happened so long before I was born, and my mother is so insistent, and the rays of that Sicilian sun beat down on my own brain so mercilessly that I find myself calling my elderly aunt, Ray's former sister-in-law, and saying . . .

"Could it be true?" I am incredulous with myself for even making this phone call, but all these voices clamor and racket in my own head, in my own life, in a busy afternoon. The Italian Mafia.

"Of course not," says my aunt. Then she backpedals to "Well, I don't *think* so."

And that is the state of mind I am more or less in on the day I receive a letter from the real Frank Balistrieri's daughter.

*I am Angela,* she says, *Mr. Balistrieri's daughter, and I have heard that your mother believes she is my father's daughter. She has my sympathy. I am married to a man who used to be in the group Sha Na Na. Like your mother, he is manic-depressive, and I think we should meet and you might like to tell my story.* Her letter falls into my hand on an afternoon like a pistol shot, and reality, whatever that may be, crashes from underneath me, a glass of amber spilling to the tavern floorboards. The writer says she lives in California, that she has been under great duress, and like my mother's writings, there is a tone in the daughter's letter that suggests that only I can save her. She says her brothers are cheating her out of the family money, that she has been through hell with her family, that she needs help. I do begin to dream of saving her, of untangling her inventory of chaos and smoothing out her delusions. I will meet her, I decide, descendants all of the big Mr. B, and then, astonishingly, I lose the letter and cannot find her again, and I wonder if I have dreamt it all. She retreats into fantasy. What a poor and puny and flickering thing is my brain—compared to hers and especially to my mother's. I cannot keep any lineage alive. I have no country. I have to invent myself, without maternity, where the winds of imagination rage so much stronger than my own.

The delusions of the brain are my territory; I specialize in them now. I am as drawn to them as to the descriptions of ancient Troy; they are a book of fairy tales I never tire of opening. When I talk to the family members of other people who have been ill, been schizophrenic or manic or heard voices, I am most eager for the stories of the magic or deception. Most of us curse ourselves secretly, believing we are so much less than what we in fact are. Whereas delusional people believe they are so much *more.*

"And I went into my father's room on the ward," says a friend, "and he announced to me that he was Jesus Christ. And what was more, he wanted me to bow down and wash and anoint his feet with oil!"

"Ah," says another, "all I had to do was serve Thanksgiving dinner to my brother, King Walla Walla Something-or-other."

The *New York Times* writes, *The suspect, thought to be mentally ill, emerged from the church where he is accused of killing the nuns, holding a trumpet and a bag of silverware.*

I clip it for my own scrapbook, fax the article to my mother. "Poor man," clucks my mother when she gets it, for I will use any cautionary tale if I think it will keep her watchful, obediently taking her lithium. And then I feel guilty, for I know there is no more harm in my mother on medication than in most of us. But I have seen the fire in her eyes. I know the ancient, primeval voices that gathered that fire. I eye the lithium pills she lays out, like Jack's beans, and look at my mother as if by taking these, she can climb to another kingdom, where it's sane. She swallows them, and defeats me.

"Got to go to work!" she smiles. "We're doing some very important work for the president! It's a secret! The Mafia's in on it, too. You know we wouldn't have this contract if it weren't for you-know-who!"

"Call me later," I say, barely looking up. I have decided this is one I can live with. Once, a woman asked my mother what her favorite early memory of my sisters and me was. She smiled. "Oh," she said, to a group of twenty people or so, "that would probably be—let's see—once I was driving these kids to Florida. The sun got brighter and brighter and brighter. Their voices got louder. The sun was so strong in my eyes, my head hurt so much, I said, 'These kids are so noisy and troublesome they're giving me a brain tumor!' " My sisters and I look at each other. It can only happen here, in this realm, in these caves, on this land.

And that is why I am going to take my mother to Italy next spring, to Sicily, to look for Frank's family. Frank Balistrieri makes her happy. His voice has never been so loud that it has given her a brain tumor. The dead man lives on in her like a lord, bestowing grace, secret power, imagined connection. I might as well make my peace, since he is, after all is said and done, crowned king of our family of the fantastic, the taproot of her brain.

---

# VERONICA CHAMBERS

There are two relationships I have with the outside world—one is with my hair, and the other is with the rest of me. Sure, I have concerns and points of pride with my body. I like the curve of my butt, but dislike my powerhouse thighs. My nose suited me fine for the last twenty-seven years. Then last week, for some strange reason, my nose seemed too big and I started to wonder about a nose job. Could I pass it off as an operation to cure my chronic sinus condition? No way would my friends fall for that, I concluded after hours of staring into the mirror. Finally, I decided it was simpler to just go back to liking my nose the way it is. My breasts, once considered too small, have been proclaimed as perfect so often that not only am I starting to believe the hype, but am booking my next vacation to a topless resort in Greece. But my hair. Oh, my hair.

I have reddish brown dreadlocks that fall just below shoulder length. Eventually, they will cover my aforementioned breasts; at which time, I will give serious thought to nude modeling at my local art school. I like my hair—a lot. But over the last eight years that I have worn dreadlocks, it has conferred upon me the following roles: rebel child, Rasta mama, Nubian princess, drug dealer, unemployed artist, rock star, world-famous comedienne and nature chick. None of which are really true. It has occurred to me on more than one occasion that my hair is a whole lot more interesting than I am.

Because I am a black woman, I have always had a complicated relationship with my hair. For those who don't know the history, here's a quick primer on the politics of hair and beauty aesthetics in the black community, vis-à-vis race and class in the late twentieth century. "Good" hair is straight and preferably, long. Think Naomi Campbell. Think Diana Ross. For that matter, think RuPaul. "Bad" hair is thick and coarse, aka "nappy" and often, short. Think Buckwheat in the Little Rascals. Not the more recent, politically correct version of *The Little Rascals,* but the old one in which Buckwheat looked like Don King's grandson.

Understand that these are stereotypes: broad and imprecise. Some will say that "good" hair and "bad" hair is outdated. And it's true, it's much less prevalent than it was in the 70s when I was growing up. Sometimes I see little girls, with their hair in braids and Senegalese twists, sporting cute little T-shirts that say HAPPY TO BE NAPPY and I get teary-eyed. I was born of the sandwich generation between the Black Power afros of the 60s and the blue contact lenses and weaves of the 80s. In my childhood, no one seemed very happy to be nappy at all.

I knew from the age of four that I had "bad" hair because my relatives and family friends discussed my hair with all the gravity that one might discuss a rare blood disease. "Something must be done," they would cluck sadly. "I think I know someone," an aunt would murmur, referring to a hairdresser with all the hushed urgency that one might refer to a medical specialist. Some of my earliest memories are of Brooklyn apartments where women did hair for extra money. These makeshift beauty parlors were lively and loud, the air thick with the smell of lye from harsh relaxer, the smell of hair burning as the hot straightening comb did its job. To this day, the smell of a hot comb crackling as it makes it way through a thick head of hair makes me feel at home. It's not so strange, some smells thrill with their boldness. I have a friend who inhales blissfully every time she puts gas into her automobile. For me, the smell of hair burning is the smell of black beauty emerging like a phoenix from metaphorical ashes: transformation.

When did I first begin to desire hair that bounced? Was it because black Barbie wasn't, and still isn't, happy to be nappy? Was it Brenda, the redhead who was my best friend in second grade? Every time she flicked her hair to the side, she seemed beyond sophistication. My hair bounced the first day back from the hairdresser's, but not much longer. My mother urged me to be careful as I played outside. "Don't sweat out that perm," she would call. But I found it impossible to sit still and not play. I think a part of me knew that it didn't matter much anyway. My hair was so thick that the perms never lasted through the end of the month. Hairdressers despaired like cowardly lion tamers at the thought of training my kinky hair. "This is some hard hair," they would say. "I'll do the best I can," they told my mother, making it clear that there were no promises to be made. As a child, I knew that I was not beautiful and I blamed it on my hair.

The night I began to twist my hair into dreads, I was nineteen years old and a junior in college. It was New Year's Eve and the boy that I longed for had not called. "We'll all meet at a club," he had said. "I'll call and tell you where." But the phone never rang. A few months before, Alice Walker had appeared on the cover of *Essence,* her locks flowing with all the majesty of a Southern American Cleopatra. I was inspired. It was my family's superstition that the hours between New Year's Eve and New Year's Day was the time to cast spells. "However New Year's catches you, is how you'll spend the year," my mother reminded me my whole life long. And so it seemed that her mantra always came true. We spent the days before New Year's cleaning our rooms, watching as our mother put clean sheets on the beds and stocked the house with groceries. On New Year's Eve, my mother tucked dollar bills into my training bra and into my brother's pants pocket so that the New Year would find us flush. The important thing on New Year's Eve was to set the stage, to make sure you kept close everything you needed and wanted. The year that we forgot to buy toilet paper, we were always running out—hollering for one another to bring to the bathroom a box of Kleenex, a roll of paper towels. The year that my father spent New Year's Eve away from home, he never returned.

Jilted on New Year's Eve, I decided to use the hours that remained to transform myself into the vision that I'd seen on the cover of *Essence* magazine. Unsure of how to begin, I washed my hair, carefully and lovingly. I dried it with a towel then opened a jar of hair grease. Using a comb to part the sections, I began to twist each section into baby dreads. My hair, at the time, couldn't have been longer than an inch. I twisted for two

hours, and in the end was far from smitten with what I saw—
my full cheeks dominated my face now that my hair lay in flat
twists around my head. The pure act of twisting my hair had
made my already short hair seem shorter. I did not look like
the African goddess that I had imagined, but it was a start. I
emerged from the bathroom and ran into my Aunt Diana, whose
headful of luxuriously long, straight black hair always reminded
me of Diahann Carroll on *Dynasty*. "Well, Vickie," she said,
shaking her head. "Well, well." I went into my room and
watched Dick Clark do the countdown in Times Square. I knew
that night my life would begin to change. I started my dreadlocks and I began the process of seeing beauty where no one
had ever seen beauty before. Like Rapunzel, I grew my hair
and it freed me, not only from perms that could never quite
tame my kinky hair down, but it freed me from a past where
my crowning glory was anything but.

There are, of course, those who see my hair and still consider
it "bad" hair. On the set of the film *Poetic Justice,* one of the
stars of the movie routinely referred to me as "Spider Head."
A family friend touched my hair recently, then said to me,
"Don't you think it's a waste? All that lovely hair twisted in
those things?" I have been asked by more than one potential
suitor if I had any pictures of myself before "you did that to
your hair." One friend was so persistent that I must have been
prettier without dreadlocks, that I wore a wig to meet him one
day. Not only did he not like me in the straight black bob that
I wore, he didn't recognize me. "I get it," he said. "Those
dreads are really you." I nodded. I have sometimes thought that
I carry all of my personality around in my head. A failure at

small talk and countless other social graces, I sometimes walk into a cocktail party and let my hair do the talking for me. I stroll through the room, silently, and watch my hair tell white lies. In literary circles, my hair brands me as "interesting, adventurous." In black middle-class circles, my hair brands me as "rebellious" or, more charitably, as "Afrocentric." In predominantly white circles, my hair doubles my level of exotica. My hair says, "Unlike the black woman who reads you the evening news, I'm not even trying to blend in."

That said, who could forget that at the end of the day, hair is just hair? "Do you think this could work out?" a man said to me recently. We sat in a tony midtown restaurant that was dark save for the flickering candlelight; in a room, almost silent, save for Billie Holiday's voice billowing above our heads as softly as smoke. Mind you, it was only our second date and I was pretty convinced that I didn't want there to be a third. "What do you mean?" I asked him, sweetly, even dumbly. "I'm very traditional and you're so wild," he said, reaching out for my hair. I wanted to bolt from my seat. "I'm not wild. You only think I'm wild," I wanted to scream. For those who are ignorant enough to think that they can read hair follicles like tea leaves, my hair says a lot of things that it doesn't mean. Taken to the extreme, my hair says that I am a pot-smoking, Rastafarian wannabe who in her off-hours strolls through her house in an African daishiki, lighting incense and listening to Bob Marley. The reality is that I don't smoke pot. That in my house, I wear Calvin Klein nightshirts and light tuberose candles that I buy from Diptyque in Paris. I play tennis in my off-hours and while I love Bob Marley, I mostly listen to jazz vocalists like Ella Fitzgerald, Diana Krall and Dee Dee Bridgewater.

I have been asked to score or smoke pot so often that it doesn't even faze me anymore. Once after a dinner party in Beverly Hills, a white colleague of mine lit up a joint. Everyone at the table passed and when I passed too, the man proceeded to cajole me relentlessly. "Come on," he kept saying. "Of all people, I thought you'd indulge." I shrugged and said nothing. As we left the party that night, he kissed me good-bye. "Boy, were you a disappointment," he said, as if I had been a bad lay. But I guess I had denied him of a certain sort of pleasure. It must have been his dream to smoke a big, fat spliff with a real live Rastafarian.

Similarly, it's such hair judgments that make me a magnet for airport security. I loathe connecting international flights in Miami and London, for I am sure to be stopped and stopped again. On a recent trip from Panama, I was stopped by five officers in one hour; each one took his time, poking through my suitcases. Finally, imprudently, I let the last officer have it. "I know what this is," I told him. "This is harassment. And it's because of my hair." He didn't even blink an eye. "We stopped them, too," he said, pointing to a group of white missionaries. "Nothing wrong with their hair." In the Bahamas, a friend and I weren't allowed into a local nightclub because as the bouncer pointed out, the sign said NO JEANS. NO SNEAKERS. NO DREAD-LOCKS. I would have laughed, if I didn't want to cry. You can change what you're wearing. How do you change the hair on your head? And why should you have to?

As much as I hate to admit it, I've been trained to turn my

head to any number of names that aren't mine. I will answer to "Whoopi." I will turn when Jamaican men call out, "Hey, Rasta" on the street. I am often asked if I am a singer, and I can only hope that I might be confused with the gorgeous Cassandra Wilson, whose dreadlocks inspired me to color my hair a jazzy shade of red. Walking through the streets of Marrakesh, I got used to trails of children who would follow me, trying to guess which country I came from. "Jamaica!" they would shout. "Ghana, Nigeria!" I shook my head no to them all. They did not believe me when I said I was from America; instead, they called me "Mama Africa" all day long. It's one of my favorite memories of the trip.

I have thought, intermittently, of changing my hairstyle. My hair is too big for me to wear hats, and I sometimes envy women with close-cropped cuts and stylish headgear. The other night, I watched one of my favorite movies, *La Femme Nikita,* and I admired Nikita's no-nonsense bob. "I couldn't be a female assassin with hair like this!" I said, jumping up out of my chair. Even pulled back, my hair is too voluminous to be so slick and stark. Then I remembered how in the movie *Coffy,* Pam Grier pulled a gun out of her Afro and I was comforted that someday, should I choose the career path of professional ass-kicker, my hair would not be an obstacle. Once, after the end of a great love affair, I watched a man cut all of his dreadlocks off and then burn them in the back-yard. This, I suspect, is the reason that might tempt me to change my hair. After all, a broken heart is what started me down this path of twisting hair. A broken heart may change my hair road. Because I do not cut my hair, I carry eight years of history on my head. One day, I may tire of this history and start anew. But one thing is for sure, whatever style I wear my hair in, I will live happily—and nappily—ever after.

# Some Praise for a Little Right-Sided Anarchy
## (That Is Also Tribute to the Lobe Girls)

## THYLIAS MOSS

Not in fifteen years had it happened, a short-lived (days) right-leg winter, an internal ice age situated in the bones. Alarming yet exciting departure from the normal whose grip sometimes gets too tight and imposes an unfortunate choke hold on the extraordinary. A deep chill is also mercilessly clean; frigid winds sweep the southernmost continent pure. Polar ice caps are like seals of approval. Some praise, then, for a little right-sided anarchy.

From toe to hip, sensation is gone and with it the awareness of half of my lap; a magazine resting on my right thigh hurts, an electrified *Science News* tries to shock the numbness out of the misbehaving nerves, but the cold darts of current are excruciating in their intensity and fury. Only napped cloth like flannel or chamois, only fleece is tolerable.[1]  My leg must be swaddled

---

[1] The word *fleece* always comforts me with the thought of the generosity of lambs. I use that word just to evoke comfort when subconsciously I am tuned to needing comfort. I think much (both frequently and highly) of this generosity, this innocent dispensation that remains in force into a sheep's maturity. An innocence retained. My ears as well are sensitive to the slightest emotional tilting out of balance, and also to my spatial location, so hearing the whisper of *fleece* inside my head restores; hearing the quiet of my thinking makes of my brain a chapel that dispenses equilibrium and renewal. As I clean my blinds by running a lamb's wool duster back and forth over them, the wool's lanolin holds the dust securely,

in it against the cutting cold of smooth percale sheets that unaffected parts of my body have not yet warmed; it must be a cushion between my skin and a piece of the thinnest onionskin paper that seems a slice of solid carbon dioxide so cold is its burn—I wince at the brutality of its weight as I persist in writing a love letter to my husband. Transfiguration is like this, sudden, without warning.

There's a chance that, eventually, the conversion will be complete. By the inch, my skin (the body's largest organ) will continue to lose sensory perception as I become outfitted in Antarctic finery, as I am primed for an absolute zero of being, becoming so cold that even in the temperate zone's snowy winters, I melt like dry ice, from solid gas to vapor. Before it dissipated, the vapor from the dry ice melting a month ago in my sink (we'd brought back frozen novelties from five hundred miles away, Wesley so crazy about lemon premium ice cream) was white with ragged edges, scored patches of fog snatched from a more widespread cloudiness in an attempted liberation of sky's preferred light and color. From my sink, stringy clouds rose, white rivers of spirochetes as I'd seen them move (making unheard pathological music) under microscopes in documentaries about Tuskeegee, but these were

---

dust composed of the notes of the music of existing, the ultimate disintegration of things into superb granular substance; to scatter dust is to release a slur of hemidemisemiquavers (sixty-fourth notes) into the air. With my wrist's motion, I am making music; the duster is like a fluffy microphone although it is my perception and imagination that are amplified, not volume or my hearing. A conductor brandishing arms, hands, and baton makes a music separate from that of the orchestral instruments: a transcending, unheard, acoustically pure song exhausting the audible high pitches and still ascending, accessing summits where sound is divinity. Sometimes I watch videos of symphony orchestras with the sound muted so as to showcase only the comfort of this effect.

benign and confined to the sky; these achieved atmospheric altitude. Bacterial and viral regiments invade silently, as if observing moments of silence to honor that which is under siege, to respect the victim (as the praying mantis seems a pious predator), to choose the host and not arbitrarily fall into an organic residence in which to proliferate quietly, reverently. It is strictly business when pathogens arrive. Suddenly, I have a cold.

The generations of virus (exceedingly more fertile than rabbits) neither celebrate victory nor accept defeat with noise as I sneeze (utilizing blaring defenses) and cough up phlegm green and yellow, for a few days, with infection. Sometimes there is also a dull aching in my ears, a pain both felt and heard; a gong distant and under water is what I hear while all through the course of the cold, the ear's external appearance remains unchanged. In my eyes, some redness, also at the tip of my nose sore from blowing; an awful nasal trumpet is what I hear especially when Wesley blows his nose to clear it of catarrh, in the process actually producing a note out of Gershwinian rhapsodies, but nevertheless, it is annoying, especially close to my ear that can't choose not to hear it. Afterwards, Wesley usually leaves a tissue stuck in his nose and asks, "Do you love me?" Do I love him at a time like this, I think, hearing those thoughts loudly and clearly; do I love him when he's behind a most inadequate veil and obviously feeling excessively comfortable around me—and then I start hearing Chaka Khan's record, *I Feel for You,* so that's what I say, "Wesley, I feel for you," as seductively as I can so he'll hear only that (for I know how consuming seduction

is, and how sensitive his ears are to both what tongues—
make that only my tongue—say and what my tongue does)
and not the layers, drowned out by seduction,[2] where I've
inserted a blank between *feel* and *you,* and where I'm listening
to myself plug into the blank all the words that can fit; I'm
really singing. And I keep singing while preparing the evening
meal, while blood drips from my not-infrequent kitchen ineptitude—no one likes to watch me handle a knife, cutting into
my knuckles when I trim asparagus stalks, blood rising to the
top of the superficial nick, rather like a Mercurochrome stain,
then almost immediately thicker and forming a suitable Ror-
schach blot on the bandage; I once thought of making a poster
(and science project) of used Band-Aid art, but was discouraged
mostly for hygienic reasons; I'd taken the wrong side in the war
to eradicate germs. There was other singing as well, the vibrato
sting of the injury, a pulsating my ear disregarded, the waves of
sting too shallow for what my ears could do: listen as Wesley
told me he knew this would happen.

   Moments and movements without sound dignify the ear just
as forfeiture of sensation exalts the leg. Everything that vibrates
yet is unheard is either infrasonic (below frequencies of sound
waves in the audible range) or ultrasonic (above frequencies in
the audible range).[3] When the audible range is bypassed, the ear

---

[2]Other than during such seduction, he is polyphonic, as hearing is designed to be, able to
hear as many sounds as are present simultaneously; pitch, location, distance, and intensity
helping the brain distinguish each sound, the waves entering the ear at different angles,
bouncing from one part of the auricle (external ear) to another before falling into the
auditory canal.

[3]Some infrasonic vibrations can be felt, however, since they occur within a range in which
some parts of the body resonate and make their own infrasonic hymns. Despite a human
tendency toward intellectual chauvinism, our hearing is quite limited among animals (eyesight

does not have to discriminate; it does not have to declare as musically sweet, uniform vibrations that set in motion the fluid in the cochlea's minute ocean where those tides are translated into impulses that are what the brain interprets; what the brain hears. Nor does the ear have to take displeasure (or delight) in more chaotic vibrations and their ruggedness, their dissonance that when allowed to intervene in melody lends the texture and complexity that improve musical compositions. The ear reprieved from making such judgments becomes a vessel strictly for maintaining balance. When its only function is balance, the ear is glorified; sound remains the result of vibration, but as if all of it is ultrasonic, all of it refined; as if only the ultrahighs survive sound's elutriation—the spirit of music camping in a sanctuary of gently vibrating leaves or in the lethargic pirouette of the ceiling fan's low-speed quiet. Such sound is not heard, but instead gives rise to awe.

The nerves of the lower half of my body after fifteen years have again (this time for a longer spell) gone insubordinate in disregarding the brain's classification of sensation. The nerves want to establish their own canon of sensation although they are the brain's own wiring, the brain's own tendrils for the relay of impulses, root hairs from a rutabaga of a brain. Or perhaps more like a cranial Portuguese man-of-war armed with masses of tentacles, the ones that extend to my right leg, toxic. These nerves stop speaking to my brain, adolescent nerves rebelling

too, as we, unlike cats, for instance, lose color perception in the dark); dolphins, bats, and cats can hear well into what for humans is the ultrasonic range, and dogs can hear both higher and lower pitches than people can hear.

and broadcasting what my brain dismisses as static, so extraordinary things happen: the open Jenn-Air oven door soothes, is icy when my right leg touches it, so cooling I don't jump from its attained 450 degrees; instead my leg photographs a ripe and spectacular (so bright and big) berry. The rush of air is a blast of menthol and mint; I am ready to do an alpine skiing ad for York Peppermint Patties.

These nerves have become tired of pleasantness; a feather one of my sons has found will torment me when he places it on my leg, drags its frozen knife-tip across my skin, and in so doing, exposes my lies to him about the incipient majesty in anything without having to turn to sadistic or masochistic explanations. *The world is song,* I've said to my sons; *listen. The ears would flap and try to fly if song had not captivated them. Consider, dear ones, that deaf ears are so captivated, they freeze, and then there is just that greatness available as echoes in a spiral in a shell's many inner chambers, a whispered "ah" that never ends.*

In the morning, it turns out that a man has had his hand on my thigh all night, and I did not know of this simple contact that was trying to be more and would have been more with encouragement I would have given to such a lovely request, the tracing of small blossoms; that is to say: the transfer of his fingertip bouquet to my skin, an invisible tattoo. I wake to a stroking that coincides perfectly with light's first and early stroking of the glass; the thin pale curtains are seductive in a way they won't be later. The light heeding the raciness of the sheerness allows shadows of birds to dive into shadows of trees, fierce and eager lovers beyond caring about an audience. I wake to a stroking that exists only visually; if the motion makes sound, it is beyond my ears' threshold of perception although it looks more intense, more vital than the whisper of his breathing that I do hear. For the first time, it seems he has touched me superficially; for the first time I resist pleasure, gratitude, tenderness, and everything else Wesley has loaded into his fingers. For the first time—although his fingers make wells in my skin, depressions around which ridges of skin rise somewhat like crowns. Ah, he still wants to make me royalty and I seem to reject it, the loss of feeling disguised as indifference. Years ago when we were falling in love, Wesley called me *princess* and my ears heard, because my brain sanctioned this elevation, the ultrasonic implications of his feelings that each day sought higher expression and made demands increasingly difficult for mere bodies to fulfill; the feelings were becoming so invested with fortitude and energy as to be able to exist without us. All unheard ultrasonic music is their song. The first time he called me *princess,* I wanted to fold the lobe of my ear up and the helix down so as to seal the actual sound inside my head, the cilia quivering always, mesmerized like the rest of me, a most rapturous form of tinnitus.[4] I imagined that if he placed his ear against mine, he would hear the resonance of his calling me and from then on would call me *honey cowry* or *concha* or *precious wentletrap.*

---

[4]Tinnitus otherwise can be maddening, I've heard, the hearing of nonexistent sound, perhaps a constant flute, a single measure of a musical piece repeated and repeated, each time further from perfection. Or a sound more harsh and equally unrelenting, wasp buzz or a wolf call at all hours, perpetual percussion: gong and cymbal, the sound of a migraine headache's pulsation pushed limbically into audibility. Some researchers believe these sounds originate in the inner ear and are boosted by the brain's limbic system which is responsible for emotions.

During the past fifteen years, this body has served me so well, I do nothing but praise it and the beautiful conspiracy of its systems. Conspiracy because what occurs within me are secretive ventures: my digestion[5] and thinking are invisible, and exactly what my eyes and ears, tongue, skin, and nose process is not necessarily disclosed; even my respiration is mostly concealed (especially under sweaters and coats) except for the intimacy of breath I share with those invited to share theirs with me, a child falling asleep in my arms, warm puffs rewarding my skin with the most sanitary of kisses, or my husband's whispering in the cinema or at dinner things for my ears only.[6] As for what is seen when I breathe in cold circumstances, that is just residue made visible by warmed exhalation colliding with winter, just carbon dioxide waste, a fibrous or cotton-candy-looking skeleton of breath. My pulse is all mine.[7]

---

[5]Excluding belches and anal flatuses that I never laughed at even when I was not the source, for the sound that reached my ear was that of a tuba, especially the attempts of a boy (that I liked) to play one. He walked home from school trying to play it, letting the tuba do all his awkward talking, its voice deeper than his would be for years. As for the odor, it was powerful but faded quickly, so hardly powerful at all—a charming little paradox. There is also the audible borborygmus which is hunger pangs or a rumbling in the intestines such as what follows the ingestion of dairy products by the lactose-intolerant.

[6]"For my ears only" yet what he says is hardly original and probably not uttered for the first time; he has loved other women and told them things for their ears only that delighted their ears probably no less (though I prefer to believe less) than my ears are delighted. It is fascinating that our secrets, our privacy, our so stunning intimacy is not unique—I cannot prove that what I hear is different from what other women have heard when he read to them the same passages of poems written by him (and by others), but I would insist that loving him has caused a reshaping of the cochlea so that his voice is brighter than any other. So too has my skin been reconfigured, its nerves reprogrammed so that his breath and touch accomplish more (except where there is anarchy). My ears are combination locks, that is to say.

[7]And that is why it is appropriate that my primary care physician or the nurse-practitioner asks if she may take it.

★   ★   ★

Thank you, body, for keeping the fifteen pounds[8] gained during my last pregnancy that was shared with a tumor trying to become as large as the baby, my baby's mute, deaf, lifeless twin; fifteen marvelous pounds that have given me a voluptuous potential I'd never earned before,[9] being in the past so lean, my legs more like reeds, carrying me always close to shorelines where herons balanced on even less than I had. The birds took off as if nothing profound had happened, as if flight were unremarkable, but the wingspan, the fully extended stole of feathers that was a more gem-like color than even buffed sapphires, provided profound evidence of conceit and the arrogance I assumed was required to kiss off gravity in the first place. I like when birds operate in higher levels of sky, advanced sky that seems unlike the colorless portion I stand within, sucking it endlessly and mostly soundlessly.

The thinner the plant by the pond, bird-leg thin, the faster it seemed to respond to silent breezes, breezes silent to me, but producing sound at levels only visual to me or only felt against my skin (it is as if waves of sound attempt to enter the body everywhere, but succeed only with the ear) that horripilates if the air moving beyond my threshold of perceiving sound is sufficiently chilled—*horripilation* is the eruption of goose bumps, an eruption that is like the score of crazy orchestration, minute

---

[8]That number again—repetitions always try to speak to me of a sacred potential, the repetition disproving accident. Symmetry is of course a form of repetition. And habits, say the habit of these footnotes, these branchings and digressions that seek to copy the anarchy of the way the arms and legs digress from the trunk, the ovaries from the uterus, the digits from the feet and hands, the ears and hair from the head.

[9]I can almost hear my hips that now are as round as bass clefs and their promise of rich sound.

brown whole notes wildly confiscating my arms. Was my first
visit to Euclid Creek also my first time envying the grass that
fluttered to air music I could not hear? Dandelion seeds would
become caught in chords, holding those notes until a descending
scale brought them to the ground where they germinated and
prepared for another sprouting. As I ran, I too set the air moving
according to my rhythms, and this the grass heard too, and this
the dandelion seeds danced to also, a fully-seeded plant in each
of my hands as I twirled, the seeds coming loose and riding in
my small spirals—a carnival of imperceptible sound; a distur-
bance of air that disturbed nothing else.

At some point, it may not be how things feel that has meaning. I will know a spoon is in my hand because I see it, because
I hear it scrape the bottom of a bowl, stir iced tea, but without
a confirmation of the logic of other senses, I won't know
whether or not a spoon has been picked up. Left will be only
abstract feeling, extrasensory love, mental orgasm, more and
more imagination. It is for love of a man that I hope the neurol-
ogists are able to help me feel again what my man wants me to
feel every day when he kisses me, when he holds me, as he sets
out to disprove the existence of inadequacy. I will still desire
him; I just won't know that I have been satisfied, but as I
always have, I will enjoy his satisfaction. I have not wanted my
satisfaction to be mine alone, but consistently I have wanted to
give it to him, to make it large enough to encompass him, to
transform a selfishness into a generosity.

At some point I may understand, better than I ever could
have without this anarchy of body, that perception is a trick.

Knowing the deception of sensation, I turn to eyes and ears, assuming that even if the whole body (including taste buds) loses the sense of touch, vision and hearing can continue and will do so more intensely. There is, however, the matter of my myopia, the distortion already present in how the world looks to me, blurry with my unaided eyes as if everything grows fur. There is clean-edged perception from six inches in front of my face to a depth of relative infinity only through corrective lenses. My ears and their no-known deficit will have to compensate. It is amazing what the body can live without successfully: limbs, sanity, movement, sight, speech, breasts, genitalia, a kidney, voice box, lung, or heart so long as there are artificial replacements. An external ear isn't absolutely essential (to lose one wouldn't necessarily impair hearing) except, really, for the cosmetic spectacle its absence creates, but hats and long hair or plastic could compensate if such eccentricity of appearance bothered the earless ones.

When I was about ten, I knew a girl, Judy, who had her ears pierced the day she turned thirteen. It was a home piercing; her aunt, another teenager, sterilized a needle in the gas stove's flame and while the needle was still hot, poked it through Judy's lobe that was already hurting from having ice cubes held against it to anesthetize it. Straws that had been singed at each end were inserted in the fresh hole to keep it open while the ear healed. She bathed her ears in alcohol and witch hazel every morning and night, but for all that rigorous nursing, something went wrong. Knobs started growing from the back of her ear, a cluster of irregular lumps, excrescences, keloids that made wearing earrings, those 14-karat gold studs she'd bought, impossible. I thought her ears would have to be amputated, but she still had them, the keloids too, two years later and the last time I saw her. Judy, although she sometimes talked to me, mostly hung out in the circle of older girls, some of whom wore earrings so humongous and heavy, they were weights that more appropriately should have been attached to wrists or ankles. These weights stretched the lobes and widened the pierced holes so tremendously, these girls could wear only pierced earrings on wires; there was nothing on which studs and earring backs could anchor. So Judy's friends kept a couple of pencils or pens in these holes. Or they carried lipsticks in these holes, rolled-up dollars, and one of them, Shaynee, hid cigarettes inside the money roll. The Famous and Fabulous Lobe Girls of the Rose of Sharon Baptist Church Young Adult Choir.

I love the perfection of Wesley's ears; it is perfection because of what has become a burnt standard, the darker rim, the top of the helix that flaming vegetable oil singed (on another night, early in our marriage, of my kitchen ineptitude) when he doused the pot with water, and only after scattering the flames (that then leaped to scorch the curtains also), thought to clamp the lid on the pot and throw it off the second-floor apartment's back porch into a bank of snow. I run my fingers along this healed rim, delighting in its flame-caused fine scallops, fluted like a tiny pie, one downsized for a mouse. Our younger son's ears were discolored from the moment of birth, all white except for the rim, the top of the helix where the ear was so dark, it seemed he had been born with scabs; the rest of his body was golden, a richly yellow tan. The white ears persisted for four months until there was a blessing of pigment—apparently drained from the scabs (they faded to tan) and redistributed.

Wesley has mild hearing deficit in the left ear; I have to get close, as I like to anyway, to speak to him on the left, where I usually am as we walk. It is mostly, however, his right ear that receives attention as my head rests through our nights on his right shoulder, as I ride as passenger in our truck. A decorative bass clef is on the side of his head. His own hyperbola—I am in love with Wesleyan geometry, the arrangement of his points, lines, and angles, and its effect upon space that I enter, that I bend and that bends me as I approach him, more supple than I am at any other time. He is a mathematical concoction, a figure that exists theoretically, in numbers; a prediction and explanation of what exists within things and makes them behave as they do, as opposed to a verifiable object. This is the calculus in which I would have excelled had I been allowed to study it when I was assigned elsewhere.

At times his ear seems a study of an embryo. In fact, acu-puncture points on the ear correspond to an understanding of the ear as an embryo. Rudimentary ears form just a few days after conception, and the cochlea completes its development before birth.[10] Wesley's ear is a map to all that he is. Its auditory canal all dark with a scant covering of cerumen (the wax that traps foreign bodies, such as insects and dust, and attempts to prevent their deeper penetration. His earwax is as moist and dark as molasses but doesn't taste sweet, whereas mine is crumbly

---

[10]Here's something else about the cochlea that I read somewhere, I think in *Newsday*: the cochleas of lesbians apparently become masculinized during gestation and are unlike the cochleas of heterosexual women; they are more like, the study found, the inner ears of men.

and barely amber) seems an ideal confessional. I love our time in bed, our voices low so that our sons hear nothing but a soothing hum, my mouth near his ear because of how he holds me, my head an egg in his nest of shoulder, and I speak into that confessional, saying everything I need to say, everything he needs to hear, filling his head with resonance.

I have said to him that his ear is a partial flower, a single petal, part of an iris, dark, as dark as the wax his ear contains, because it is night and I can't see color anymore. His ear is a night flower; it blooms only at night; it unfolds and releases a powerful fragrance that lures the nocturnal bugs, me among them, seeking that Aqua Velva bite and nectar.

There are night-blooming botanical rarities that many people have never seen, rarities for which it is worth losing sleep to hurry sundown and see the pale flowers open for the luna and white-lined sphinx moths, all of the moon flowers opening at once, the sounding of gauze trumpets, a unison oh so remarkable, unified to a ten-thousandth of a second. When they open, I open my body to Wesley, unified to that same ten-thousandth.[11]

---

[11] I remember a girl I read about once—I think her name was Katie—who depended upon such night shows, who can never be a sun worshipper because untraviolet radiation (the visible spectrum is not a problem—except that it is part of the electromagnetic range of sunlight) blisters and ulcerates her skin; light is fatal to her, so hers is the world of shadow, the quieter world when most things sleep, as if light also controls volume. Crickets seem more powerful at night, their voices more urgent. The sound of owls emerges, sound of wolves, sound of the settling of wood, sound of single drops of water, of my mother calling me home, as she used to (my bedtime), from many miles away; even the sound of caterpillars still polishing off in unison at dusk the needles of evergreen shrubs and the young May leaves becomes more pronounced. In the darkness is the enhanced demarcation of sound, is Katie's concert. In the moonlight is Katie's vacation, in the evening is her triumph over xeroderma pigmentosum (her extreme light sensitivity); in the evening is the rising of her award of the precious silver medal with its many maria, all those splendid shelters from illumination, black heavens. She loves the ahs, depends on the hushes.

Each day he comes home, from the office, to the only comfort that sustains him, to a castle ruled by symbiosis. Now that numbness again is part of this royal treatment, that sweet man checks my bath, testing the water since today I perceive only coolness, relief, paradigms of beneficient expression—and nothing else in all the world.

---

# FRANCINE PROSE

What a privileged position the nose occupies in the body! Front and center on our faces, poking into the world. If the eyes are the mirror of the soul, the nose must be the soul's doorknob. The figurehead on the prow of the body's ship. The hood ornament on the car.

What is it doing there, anyway? Breathing, without making a point of itself, without—for all its forwardness—getting in the way, its respiratory function acknowledged, but most often taken for granted, not generally considered unless the nose gets a cold and becomes a nuisance demanding our unceasing care, obedience and attention.

Anatomy books remind us of the nose's protective qualities, its critical role as the guardian of our delicate airways. An aerodynamic filtration system, a muffler processing the exhaust from the huge toxic engine of the roaring life outside us.

Here is the language of physiology—on the subject of the nose—taken from the fifteenth edition of *Anatomy and Physiology,* by Kimber, Gray, Stackpole, Leavell, Miller and Chapin.

*The nose is the special organ of the sense of smell, but it also serves as a passageway for air going to and from the lungs. It filters, warms and moistens the entering air and also helps in phonation. . . . Under normal conditions breathing should take place through the nose. The arrangement of the conchae makes the upper part of the nasal passages very narrow; these passages are thickly lined and freely supplied with blood, which keeps air temperature relatively high and makes it possible to moisten and warm the air before it reaches the lungs. The hairs at the entrance to the nostrils and the cilia of the epithelium serve as filters to remove particles which may be carried in with the inspired air.*

But that doesn't quite explain it all, does it?

The authors of *Anatomy and Physiology*—Nurses Kimber, Gray, Stackpole, Leavell, Miller and Chapin—do not, for example, conjecture about what would happen if one woke up in the morning and discovered one's nose had absconded.

Gogol did, of course. In his story "The Nose," the barber Ivan Yakovlevich is biting into his breakfast roll when he discovers that the filling—"something whitish"—is none other than the recognizable(?!) nose of his regular customer, Collegiate Assessor Kovalev. Just as the barber is dropping the errant nose off the bridge (what else could he do with it?) he's stopped by the police, but before we can learn the outcome of this, we are transported to Kovalev's bedroom where he has just discovered that the pimple on his nose is gone—and so is his nose.

A self-promoting social climber and a ladies' man, Kovalev is the last guy who wants to go around noseless. Alarmed, he hurries out into the streets of St. Petersburg, where he finds his nose in the cathedral, all dressed up, the nose's "face completely concealed by his high stand-up collar, and he was praying with an expression of the utmost piety."

Confronted, the nose high-handedly denies his relation to his former owner, and returns to his prayers. Kovalev tries in vain to place a "missing nose" ad in the newspaper, where the maddening sympathetic clerk offers the noseless man a pinch of snuff. At last a policeman returns the nose, which has been caught getting onto a stagecoach for Riga, bearing the passport of a government official, of whom the nose was apparently doing a convincing imitation. But even with the doctor's minis-trations, the nose refuses to be stuck back on Kovalev's face. One morning, Kovalev wakes up to find that the nose has coop-eratively just reappeared in the middle of his face, and the major goes back to his old life, as if nothing had happened.

Like Gregor Samsa's metamorphosis into the giant insect, Kovalev's separation from, and reunion with, his nose is made to seem entirely plausible: a perhaps surprising but really (when you think of it) quite everyday occurrence. Despite the Three Stooges tone of ditsy peculiarity assumed by certain of Gogol's unnamed narrators, or "authorial" voices, Gogol himself was a careful writer. Which means that if he said *nose,* he meant *nose,* and not any other organ. Still, more than enough weird sexual anxiety suffuses the story (including, for example, a disturbing scene in which Kovalev writes a letter blaming the mother of a girl he has been courting for the loss of his nose) so that one has to at least *consider* the psychosexual readings of the story— arguments that the nose is a stand-in for Kovalev's (and Gogol's) genital preoccupations.

Is the nose a sexual organ? The perfume industry thinks so,

and consumers spend fortunes yearly at least partly in the fond hope that they are buying some sort of bottled aphrodisia, straight or watered down. Shalimar, Opium, Obsession—the names conjure up the druggy somnolence of sex, the mystical lascivious lure of the "Oriental."

Wilhelm Fliess, an early associate and friend of Freud's (Freud was for years a passionate admirer of Fliess and had one of his most spectacular attacks of travel anxiety while parting from Fliess at the Berchtesgaden station), devoted considerable time and energy to exploring the nose's role as a sexual barometer. In 1897, the Berlin nose and throat doctor published his discovery of the "nasal reflex," based on his observation that the nasal tissues swell during sexual arousal and menstruation. "It comprises headache, neuralgic pains widely distributed . . . and, thirdly, disturbances of the internal organs, of the circulation, respiration and digestion—a very wide net. *The point about the syndrome was that all the manifestations could be relieved by applying cocaine to the nose.* [Italics mine.] Its cause was either organic (after results of infection, etc.) or functional—vasomotor disturbances of sexual origin." This last feature linked with Freud's investigations, more especially since the Fliess syndrome bore the plainest resemblance to neurasthenia, one of Freud's "actual neuroses." (Ernest Jones, *The Life and Work of Sigmund Freud,* page 290.) Their friendship, conducted mostly in letters and in meetings that the half-jokingly called "congresses," lasted for a decade until the two men had a falling-out in 1900; afterwards, Fliess would resist Freud's attempts to revive their connection. And Freud would again demote the nose to its properly humble station.

*       *       *

Poor nose! Never getting its due! Our unheralded protector! The unsung organ of taste, a sense which we locate unfairly in the mouth and the tongue until the nose's temporary blockage compels us to notice that something essential is missing. How soon we forget that experiment in grade school or junior high science when our teachers persuaded us to shut our eyes and hold our noses and we discovered that we could not tell the difference between an apple and an onion. Wine-lovers, of course, know better—hence the ritual sniffing, the use of the terms "bouquet" and, yes, "nose." As do fishmongers and prudent grocery shoppers who know that sniffing is the closest we can get to a sure test of a melon's ripeness. (One of the horrors of shrink-wrapped supermarket produce is the barrier it puts between our—prospective—food and our noses.)

If we focus on the nose, everything falls into place. Certainly it is possible to read the history of imperialism and capitalism as the story of the triumph of the small, thin, delicate nose over the larger and more fleshy one. So in our culture, so heavily influenced by the Teutonic and the Northern European, we grow up associating certain characteristics with certain sorts of noses—the cute, the pert, the attractive, with all that cuteness and pertness implies about the virginal and the pure. While the "lower" forms of humanity, the Third World and the Semitic, betray their unbridled, lustful, sensual natures with their thicker or longer noses.

If the various sins reside in various parts of the body—gluttony in the stomach, lechery in the genitals and the brain, grabby envy and greed in the mouth and the hands—then vanity, I would suggest, resides at least part-time in the nose.

Consider, if you will, the power of a pimple on the tip of

the nose as opposed to a much larger blemish anywhere else on the face. Children recognize that the red nose of the clown is a comical apparatus, as opposed to nearly any other imaginable distortion of the "ordinary" facial features—for example, a jagged scar running across the forehead.

And no one has yet written a version of *Cyrano de Bergerac* in which the feature that disqualifies the hero from being a possible—a conceivable—candidate for his beloved's affections is a weak or wobbly chin, or close-together eyes. Indeed, his oversized nose is so central to Cyrano's nature (and his dilemma) that the passage we remember best in the play (far better than any of the love scenes) is our hero's aria on the subject of the curious and rude responses that his nose has evoked.

Contemplating the subject of "the nose," I seem to have recovered a memory dating from several decades before I'd ever heard the phrase "passive-aggressive"—years before that mystifying oxymoron came into common usage. Nonetheless, there was an extremely passive-aggressive girl in my class at the small private school that I attended from the fourth grade until my senior year in high school.

The smallness of the school created a fierce sense of belonging and exclusion, comforting to those who belonged, a torment to those who didn't. New kids, by definition, did not belong. I remember spending my first year there—squandered a year of my childhood—waiting for the year to pass, so I wouldn't be new anymore, and some other kids would be new.

The nose-related memory occurred in the sixth grade, and the effect that it had on me can be seen in the clarity with which I remember it, since I find myself forgetting so much that happened last week. The event took place in art class, the only class in which we were allowed to talk. My passive-aggressive classmate was telling me—or pretending that she was telling me—how much everyone liked me, how well I fit into the school, though I had been there only two years, as opposed to the eternity of having been there since kindergarten.

She told me that most of the students in the class agreed: they could hardly remember when I was the new kid. But she, as it happened, *did* remember: how astonished she and our classmates had been when they met me for the first time—This little kid with a huge nose. That was what she recalled.

*This little kid with a huge nose?* Why had I never noticed? It wasn't as if I hadn't subjected ever inch of my face and body to the most intense and criticial scrutiny. And yet somehow I'd missed the fact that my nose was any larger than anyone else's. I don't suppose I'd bothered scrutinizing myself in profile. In fact, my nose had looked quite normal to me, perhaps because my father, whom I adored, had a nose far larger than mine. Consequently, I'd assumed that my own was in the small-to-normal range.

I remember running to the mirror, as one does at such moments. My classmate wasn't making it up. I did indeed have a huge nose, though I was no longer a little kid; in addition to my other griefs, I'd grown taller than most boys my age.

My nose had increased in advance of the rest of me—and then capriciously outgrown me: nose attached to a neck and shoulders, a torso, arms and legs. The rest of me had vanished. My nose was the only thing in the mirror. For years after that

I imagined my nose as much larger than it was: an alien leviathan that had taken over my body.

Other girls were getting nose jobs, transformations that took place during mysterious disappearances over school vacations from which they returned looking vaguely porcine, or else like Lon Chaney in *The Phantom of the Opera*. Some divine and miraculous intercession kept me from seriously considering altering the shape or dimensions of my (as I thought then) enormous nose. Or maybe it was sheer cowardice, springing from the descriptions I'd read of the process by which the plastic surgeon breaks your nose and reassembles it again.

How I would have missed the feature which I've come to love best, with a kind of late-blooming narcissism that drew me into an intense admiration for my least conventional feature. Or perhaps it was the realization that the women I thought were most beautiful—Maria Callas, Anna Magnani, that Italian aristocrat with the magnificent nose in the Richard Avedon photograph—had noses that were sizable, bold, that insisted on their right to exist.

It seems our noses do protect us. Several months ago, as I was leaving my hotel room in an old-fashioned French country hotel, I went back for something I'd left in the room and ran smack into the glass door which (for some obscure reason having to do with French country charm) stood in front of the wooden door in the dimly lit lobby. I hit the door so hard that if my nose hadn't been there to intercede on my behalf, I would most likely have suffered a concussion.

The pain was so intense that I thought at first that I'd broken my nose, but as it turned out, I'd only managed to break the skin in a neat inverted vee over the bony crown. I applied an ice pack, then covered the wound with a Band-Aid—a small Band-Aid did the trick. Yet my injury seemed to me so public, so obvious that I felt like a huge, walking, talking neon bandage stickered to (and steering) its own teensy head and body.

Once more, it made me realize how attached, so to speak, I am to my nose. How I've learned to treasure it, though I may not be mindful of how hard it's working, how much it's doing for me. Looking out for me, I should say. How shocked and devastated I would be to wake up on some otherwise ordinary morning to find that my nose had vanished from my face and reappeared, all the way across town, in someone else's breakfast.

_____

## LYNDA BARRY

My cousin Huggy rolled into town on his way to Mexico to get his teeth pulled and I was glad he was getting his teeth pulled because they were saggy teeth, very loose and rotten and wobbling like wet blue socks on a clothesline and they gave him breath straight from the vents of hell.

I was pouring him fat shots of Wild Turkey, hoping that the sterilizing powers of alcohol might stem the bacteria gasses so I could concentrate on what he was saying. And as usual he was laying his conflagrating questions on me, asking me what I thought the teeth of Jesus looked like.

I said, "Huggy, I haven't thought about it much."

He said, "Cousin Bill, have you thought about it once ever? You ever once stopped to wonder why in all the pictures you've seen of him, his teeth are never showing?"

I said, "Huggy, I sure am glad you are going to Mexico."

He said, "For what I want, I _have_ to go to Mexico."

And then he started asking me about the teeth of evil. What I thought they looked like. If I was going to describe the devil's teeth how would I do it? And so the discussion ran to fangs and rot and Dracula.

Huggy said, "You ever wondered why it's so easy to describe the teeth of evil and impossible to describe the teeth of Jesus?"

I poured him another binger. "I don't think it's impossible."

He downed it. "Do it. Tell me what you think they look like."

"You know, regular teeth. Decent teeth."

"Good teeth?"

"Uh-huh."

"Perfect teeth?"

"Pretty close."

"How close?"

And then the discussion ran to overbites and slight gaps and rotated eyeteeth. Huggy kept throwing out possible flaws and I kept saying, no, no, uh-uh, no.

Huggy said, "How about a broken front tooth? Or front teeth missing altogether?"

"I can't imagine that."

"What about no teeth, then?"

"Naw."

"How about on the devil? No teeth on the devil. He opens his mouth and it's all gums."

"I don't think so."

"Then dentures."

"On the devil?"

"On b-b-bosh of them."

When Huggy drinks he develops a lateral lisp and a stutter, and when he gets excited the spit goes flying.

"C-caaaaan you pishure d-d-denshures on J-j-jeshush?"

I shook my head.

"C-c-can you pishure them on m-m-me?"

"Huggy, you'll be one handsome bastard with new teeth."

"You r-r-remember when J-j-johnny Casch got h-h-his teesch pulled? Why are you p-p-putting the c-cap back on that b-bottle? Keep p-pouring, you t-tight schonnuvvabish!"

And the night went on like that, we talked about Johnny Cash's natural teeth versus his dentures, same with George Jones and Loretta Lynn and the list went on and on. "Oncsh they m-make it t-to Naschville th-they all g-g-get the schame damn teeth." He said the new teeth ruined the music of their faces. At least I thought that's what he said before he threw up on my kitchen floor.

He left the next morning on a beat-to-hell Kawasaki. He said, "Which way's Mexico?" I pointed my finger south and mentioned something about how he could trade up to a better bike with the money he was going to save.

"I'm not going to Mexico to save money."

"Vacation."

"Hell no."

"What, then?"

"They got dentists down there who understand a man's need for customized teeth."

"Uh-huh. Meaning what?"

He pulled out a picture of Guy Clark standing in a parking lot holding a can of Lone Star beer and wearing a cowboy hat. His teeth looked pretty assorted, with a twisted eyetooth recessed deep.

"These here are the ones. Just like these."

I squinted through my hangover haze. I said, "Because you like the music of his face."

Huggy said, "Music of his face? What the hell are you talking about?"

A couple of months went by and the conflagrating question concerning the teeth of Jesus stayed in my mind. I decided Guy Clark's teeth would look fine in the mouth of Jesus and if there was such a thing as the music of a face, Guy Clark's teeth would keep it there.

Then the phone rang and it was Huggy shouting at me from a pay phone in Sturgis, South Dakota. He was at the fiftieth annual Black Hills Motorcycle Classic. "Couschin Bill! G-get your dumb asch d-down here! You never scheen anything like it! People boarding up their windows like there'sh a hurricane coming! Three-hunnred-pound men with baby chihuahuash in m-matsching outfitsh! Schaw a stuffed r-rat shtrapped to a bald man'sh head and it wash g-g-giving the finger! Ish your k-kind of placesh, B-bill!"

And so I went. And I combed through 200,000 people in search of my cousin who was not where he said he would be at all. I met a group of bikers for Jesus who handed me a religious tract that began with *He would have ridden a Harley*. I never heard of bikers for Jesus before but in Sturgis there were thousands of them. They had booths where you could buy Christian biker merchandise and that is where I saw a painting called *The Laughing Jesus*.

Huggy was so right. I couldn't believe how right Huggy was about the teeth of Jesus. The ones the artist painted on him were bright and flawless and they made Jesus look completely insane. He would never have had teeth like that, no one in this world should have teeth like that.

Huggy flipped his bike during the rally. He flipped his bike and he went up and just never came down. By the time I got there he was two days gone. I found out when I called his brother Dale, the successful one, to see if he might know anything about where Huggy disappeared to. I held the pay phone receiver hard against one ear and put my finger in the other and told Dale he was going to have to shout. He must have said it five times before I understood.

It was me who identified the body and oversaw its transport home. I carried back the plastic sack that contained his wallet and a few other things from his pockets. Keys, a couple of quarters. They didn't find his lower plates but his uppers were there.

I'm sure there are people who will think it was sick of me to keep them, but I knew they were just going to get thrown out. The funeral was closed casket and even if it wasn't, the mortician wouldn't have used them. They have wax forms that work better to make a dead man's lips lay more naturally than teeth ever would.

Huggy didn't get the teeth of Guy Clark after all. The teeth the Mexican dentist made for him were shaped exactly like his old ones were, gapped and scraggly and chipped but looking so clean and healthy and alive. Teeth that would give music to the face of anyone. To God, man, or the devil himself.

# ESMERALDA SANTIAGO

My skin is richly toned, soft brown, *trigueña* we say in Puerto Rico, wheat-colored. Not white, not black, *trigueña* is not a race. It is a blend of all the races that have contributed to my brownness. *Trigueña* is what, in the United States, makes me "Other."

There are spots on my *trigueña* skin, birthmarks and scars, blemishes, wrinkles, veins that refuse to be contained in deeper tissue and have made their way to just below the surface. I often find unexplained bruises on my limbs, dark blue, angry splotches that turn purple before they fade. Below my eye there is a red dot that appeared one day, a punctuation to something I saw, perhaps. On my neck, around my torso there are small chocolate brown tags that materialized during my first pregnancy. Or maybe they were always there and I didn't notice them before. Lately they seem to be creeping toward my face, and I imagine it is the darker me emerging, taking over the lighter skinned Esmeralda. Maybe I'm becoming other than "Other."

I need not look hard to read history etched on my skin. There, along the arch of my left foot, is the scar left when I stepped on the sharp barbs of a wire fence. On the outside of my left knee is another scar, formed when a nail that protruded from the balusters of our porch cut a deep wedge that took weeks to heal. A smile hovers over my pubic hair, the wound through which doctors delivered my two children. Right in the center of my forehead is a dash, all that remains of the bloody mess when Chago, my childhood playmate, threw a rock that found its mark. That scar has been swallowed by the deep wrinkles left by surprise and worry.

Each line, each spot, each scar is a story, forgotten by almost everyone else involved, but not by me. That scar on top of my foot? It was not an accident, as I told Mami. We were living in the city, in two rooms behind a bar. My brother Raymond's foot had been injured in an accident—my fault, I thought, because I'd been left in charge and wasn't careful enough. Raymond, then four years old, was in and out of hospitals for weeks. Nights, he cried because his foot hurt so much. Days, he limped, and whimpered pitifully with every step. Doctors thought he'd never heal and that he should be amputated.

Curled at the edge of my foot, my smallest toe looked silly and useless. I pinched it, stuck pins into it, placed it under the metal leg of a chair, then pressed hard with all my weight. It hurt, but not nearly as much as I thought it should, and it didn't bleed. Raymond's foot bled, and angry bubbles of pus formed around the wound the doctors cleaned again and again.

One day, while Mami was outside de-feathering a chicken, I went into the bedroom, rummaged through her sewing box, and found the heavy scissors she took to work in the bra factory. They were black and silver, weighed on my hand solid and menacing. They were very sharp, and I was certain they could slice through that useless little toe in a neat cut.

I straddled the windowsill, my left leg dangling outside, my right knee pressed up to my chest. It was mid-afternoon, and shadows crept from one end of the yard to another. I held the scissors, cool to the touch, opened and closed them a couple of times as if they were jaws. I was not afraid. I'd been cut, scraped, or bruised hundreds of times. My skin was, even then, spotted with scars on every limb. They had all been accidents, but this was the first time I deliberately hurt myself.

I placed the sharp blades of the scissors around my toe and squeezed the handle, but didn't have the strength to cut clear through. The skin opened and a bubble of blood sprouted then trickled down to my sole. It hurt, but not nearly enough. I hopped down from the windowsill, was about to put the scissors away and take care of the wound when I noticed how my bare feet provided a perfect target. I dropped the scissors, point down, an inch above my middle toe. It hurt more than I could have imagined, and I screamed and hopped around as the scissors twinked onto the cement floor. Everyone came running. Mami, her hands and hair clumped with chicken feathers. My sisters and brothers, who had been playing in the shadows under the mango tree. Even Raymond limped over, and screeched when he saw the blood spurt from my foot, the same foot that hurt him so much.

Mami took care of it right away, so the wound didn't fester, and there was no threat that my foot would be amputated. But it hurt a lot, almost as much, I thought, as Raymond's must have. The scar that was left is round, less than a quarter inch in diameter, a tiny crater where I store guilt.

An active child will get hurt, a competitive one will hurt others. I was both, and my skin confirms the many falls and tumbles of a childhood in motion. I never broke a bone, but scrapes, cuts, stings, and punctures have left their mark on me, and I have inflicted them on others. My ten sisters and brothers can each point to what's left of the arguments that turned into fights that drew blood.

I was eighteen when I chased my brother Héctor up the stairs. I caught up to him on the top step, reached out, grabbed a handful of his hair, and yanked. We tumbled down, causing a racket that brought my mother, stepfather, grandmother, her boyfriend, my nine other sisters and brothers, and a neighbor to the hallway, where Héctor and I lay sprawled, punching one another. Mami pulled us apart, yelled at me that as the eldest, I should stop acting like a little kid, and at Héctor that at four-teen and almost a man, he should not hit girls. I threw one last punch, and so did he, and we had to be separated again. I stumbled off, blood dribbling down my leg, a thin red ribbon from a gash below my knee.

I don't remember what Héctor said or did that made me chase him up the stairs, and probably neither does he. But I'm reminded of that humid afternoon every time I shave my legs because there is a round, flat scar on my right shin, its surface lighter than the skin around it. On that scar there is no hair, just as now, thirty-two years later, there is no hair atop Héctor's head. Within the uneven borders of the scar on my shin I hold the course of time, the physical changes it has wrought on me and my loved ones.

In my rural childhood, toys were not purchased, they were made. As children, we sought Y-shaped branches of various sizes, set them to dry and harden in the hot Puerto Rican sun. A discarded bicycle inner tube cut into strips made the perfect tensile straps and cradle for a slingshot. A battered bucket was my first target, the pings of a hit resonating with a satisfying echo that no one could argue with. As I gained skill, the targets became smaller—a bottle, a tomato sauce can, a mango still on its branch.

Not allowed to wear pants, I insisted Mami put pockets in the cotton dresses she made for me and my sisters so that I could carry pebbles in them. The sash at my waist that tied into a bow in the back of the dresses held the slingshot at my side, and I practiced drawing it out like a cowboy a six-shooter. No one could outdraw me, or outshoot me.

An iguana scurrying into the shade of the annatto bushes had no chance against me. A bird in mid-flight would plummet to the ground, stunned by a well-aimed rock. Snakes slithering under piles of kindling for the stove, lizards scuttling from branch to branch on the avocado tree, mice scampering toward the kitchen—not one reached their goal. Their death came as a soft hiss through the humid air followed by a sharp thwack to their narrow heads.

"Girls shouldn't play with slingshots," the neighbors muttered, but if I killed the rat that ate into their sack of rice, they sent Mami a bowl of candied papaya or a bagful of fresh pigeon peas.

It was a well-aimed slingshot stone that left a scar I never see. My neighbor and playmate, Chago, claimed to have seen an *ardilla,* a Puerto Rican mongoose, in the hill behind his house. We set out to hunt it, but on the way down the road we got into an argument about who was the best shot. Everyone knew I was, and I reminded him of this, but his response was to mumble *"Tu madre,"* under his breath. *Mencionar la madre,* to mention another person's mother as a curse, is a major insult in Puerto Rico, and I did what anyone would have done. I punched him in the mouth. After he recovered from the surprise of a girl striking out, he backed up, bent over, picked up a fist-size rock, and threw it at me. I fell on my face, my forehead covered in blood. As he ran off, he called out a few more specific insults about my mother. When he looked back to see if I was following him, a stone from my slingshot found its mark, square on his left eye. The scar I never see was formed when doctors sewed his eyelid shut. And while there were welts left after the beating administered by my mother, who did not care I was defending her when I shot Chago's eye out, they healed soon after we moved from the barrio. The scar Chago left on me closed into a hyphen that divides and connects the right side of my face from the left. Inside it I store power.

Another scar invisible to me was found by a hairdresser. WALK-INS WELCOME the sign on the window of Tami's Hair and Nails stated. Inside was Tami herself, redheaded, green-eyed, long orange nails in the shape of spades. She tried to talk me out of cutting my waist-length hair. "If I cut it to shoulder length," she offered, "it will be enough of a change." It had taken over seven years to grow, seven years in which I fell in love with, and was betrayed by, a man who loved my long hair. "I want it really short," I insisted. Tami gathered a long ponytail at the base of my neck, tightened a rubber band around it, and cut. The strands that were freed from the weight of the hair below the cut line came to attention into a fuzzy halo around my face. "More," I ordered. "Chop it all off."

"Boy," Tami giggled, "you must be really mad at him."

The more she cut, the more liberated I felt, until she stopped, gently tipped my head forward, and parted the stubble. "Oh, honey," she murmured, "this must have hurt." She traced a line from just above the nape of my neck toward the crown of my head.

That one was caused by my mother. Quique and I had been discovered behind the outhouse with our hands on each other's private parts. His mother used a switch that left puffy red stripes on his legs and back. But Mami grabbed the first thing she could get her hands on, a cast-iron frying pan. She chased me around the yard, screaming that I had no shame. Inside the scar she left on the back of my head I store desire.

The scars on my skin are only the most painful traces of my life. There are also the stamps I was born with, the freckles that dot my cheeks and nose, the birthmark shaped like the island of Hispaniola that floats just under my navel, the dark dot on the back of my neck that I thought was sexy. Those birthmarks are my disappointment. Why do I have freckles? Why did no lover ever kiss that spot on the back of my neck?

As a child fascinated with geography, I loved the fact that the middle of the Greater Antilles was represented on my belly. I searched for Cuba and Puerto Rico, but neither was visible on my skin. Superstitious enough to believe anything, I thought the birthmark meant that someday I was destined to live in Santo Domingo or Port au Prince. But when I did leave Puerto Rico, it wasn't for another island. I studied a map of the United States, wondering which had the same shape as the birthmark under my navel. None do, but I'm still superstitious enough to believe there is some significance to it, some reason why the shape of the island near my navel looks like Haiti and the Dominican Republic but not Puerto Rico. I've concluded that it is because I will die there. Within the ragged borders of that birthmark I hold fear.

My cousin Corazón has a birthmark on the inside of her right knee. It is round, chocolate brown, the size of a plain M&M. I once asked her about it, and she told me her mother wished for it when she was pregnant, and that's why Corazón was born with one. I didn't believe her, so I asked her mother.

"There is a reason," Titi Ana said, "that it's called a *lunar*."

When she was pregnant with Corazón, Titi Ana confessed to her midwife that if her child were a girl, she wished she would have a birthmark near her lip, just like Maria Félix, the Mexican movie star. The midwife assured Titi Ana that the moon would not deny a pregnant woman an *antojo,* and told her what she had to do to make her wish come true. Titi Ana followed the midwife's instructions, but at the last minute, realized that the birthmark might not look as good near the lip if the child were a boy. So she wished for it where it would be invisible to everyone else. Titi Ana could not have predicted that someday Corazón would wear miniskirts and that people would compliment her on the moon-shaped dark spot near her knee.

Years later, when I became pregnant and modern medicine assured me I was having a girl, I remembered Titi Ana's story, and decided to test the moon. Would it fulfill my wish for a pretty *lunar* on my daughter? Titi Ana had died years earlier, but I'd never forgotten her soft voice repeating the midwife's instructions for ensuring a birthmark on a child.

On the seventh month of my pregnancy, I stepped outside on the first night of a full moon. "You must invite the spirit of a woman in your family to help you," Titi Ana had said, and so I closed my eyes and called upon her, until I felt her presence, cool and silent near me. My hands on my belly, I rubbed circles counterclockwise, spoke to my child until I felt her moving. "Tonight you will receive a gift," I said, "from the moon and from your Great-aunt Ana, who watch over you."

I faced the moon, opened my eyes, and was about to put my right index finger near my lip when, like Titi Ana before me, I worried that a *lunar* would not look good there. I changed my mind, but then it occurred to me that, now that I was outside, facing the full moon, having summoned both my un-born child and the ghost of Titi Ana, I had to make a wish because spirits didn't like to be disturbed for no reason at all. If I didn't make a wish, it might mean bad luck for my daughter. I pressed the tip of my index finger halfway up my left thigh, and wished for a *lunar* there, a much more intimate place than where Corazón has hers. Two months later, when Ila was born, she had a dark chocolate birthmark on the inside of her left thigh. As soon as the doctors saw it, they took a biopsy, and on subsequent exams, her doctor has studied it, measured it, scraped the center of it, concerned it might be malignant.

But it's not a precancerous lesion. It is a gift from me, Titi Ana, and the moon, a spot where Ila can gather knowledge of the mysteries of woman.

When I stand naked before a mirror, I see how skin has evolved from the tight, firm, bouncy sheath that held me in, to the looser, softer, more textured canvas on which I sketch my life. Except for the ones I was born with, there are no marks on my skin that have not come from experience. But even the birthmarks and freckles on my body have meaning, imposed on them by superstition.

Wrinkles, engraved time on my skin, reveal themselves in unexpected ways at surprising times. I noticed the lines across my forehead as a teenager, after reading an article in *Glamour* magazine. As the writer instructed, I faced the mirror to determine if I had dry, oily, or combination skin, and there they were, two faint inverted vees over my eyebrows, and one line that ran temple to temple above the scar left by Chago's rock. When I looked closer, there were more; two tiny vertical lines where my nose met my forehead, two more beside my lips.

It was the first time I realized that I was not just growing up, I was growing old. Old like my grandmother and the man who owned the candy store. Old like my social studies teacher and the school principal. Old like my uncle Chico and great-aunt Chía. The first signs of mortality were etched on my skin, faint but visible, wrinkles formed by an often too expressive face. Should I stop frowning, smiling, squinting, puckering my lips? No, the beauty magazines only advised I moisturize.

Years later, and in spite of thousands of dollars spent on beauty products that promised to keep the skin on my face looking younger, firmer, more supple, I am wrinkled. Were I to slather moisturizer on every part of my body, my skin might not reveal its fifty years. But would moisturizer keep away the wrinkles I recently noticed around my breasts? How about the folds over my knees, and over my elbows? Would several more thousand dollars have erased the deep lines around my neck? The beauty industry would say yes. Plastic surgeons would argue that a nip here, a tuck there, would accomplish more than truckloads of creams. I could look twenty years younger, they promise.

Twenty years! I can erase the wrinkles caused by the final frantic days before my wedding. The puffy folds around my eyes can be cut away, so that it looks as if I never cry. The saggy skin around my breasts can be excised, eradicating three years of nursing babies. The skin around my middle can be tucked so as to deny the pregnancies, the distention caused by too many rich meals, the aversion to sit-ups.

But what about the scars? Would they too be erased? Where would I hide despair? Would each and every birthmark locate to a different spot now that the skin has been pulled, nipped, pinched? What do I do with superstition? And if these new scars, the ones created by plastic surgery, the ones that will erase experience from my body, come to me while I'm unconscious on an operating table, what will they contain?

★    ★    ★

My skin scars easily, but it also heals fast. It has been an advantage in life, this skin that has taken such abuse but still responds to a caress. In spite of all the scars, or maybe because of them, I'm thin-skinned and sensitive. This skin that has held me in but has loosed so much it's had to fold into itself, still feels, still bleeds, still stores who I am, have been, hope to become. *Trigueña,* wrinkled, spotted, bruised, marked, and scarred, my skin is the surface on which I read sorrow, superstition, the passage of time. Its texture, color, and tone have changed over the years, but within its confines I have survived a half century of life, each moment indelibly carved into my flesh.

# NATALIE KUSZ

I know some things about scars. I know how, as a jagged tear mends, it hurts more ferociously, pulls apart more easily, in the end hardens up more unevenly than a straight cut, say from a tin can or a scalpel. I know how hair won't grow in a scarred spot, or not in any respectable way, just a strand or two here or there, and these often mutant.

I know that a vitamin E capsule, punctured and rubbed on a scar every day, will fade the red tissue to a soft pink or white. I know that a scar can sunburn.

I know that deep-tissue scars are harder, more sinewy, than shallow ones, and I know how in a broad patch, after a day in the sun, you can sometimes see capillaries with your naked eye. I know, even so, that a scar's blood supply is minimal, and that if you rub one open it hardly bleeds, just turns a little slimy and pink. I know that the scab on a reopened scar is very smooth, very thin, more like a dried-out spot on raw steak than any crust you'd pick off a skinned knee.

I know that even old scars will itch, and that you should slap them hard rather than scratch them, because once you tear them back open they take a long time—once, for me, it was years—to heal shut again. I know that if you gain weight (I have grown very fat since my first major injuries) a scar will stretch some, but after a point it stays put while the flesh pushes up around it. Related to this, I know that Americans find scars and body fat equally unappetizing, so a large scarred woman is doubly handicapped, glamour-wise.

I know, as I say, some things.

But whatever I know relates to scars that make sense, ones which are the end results of healing, desirable and wholesome and inert. I learned these things first during childhood, after sled dogs tore me apart, when those wounds and the surgeons' cuts festered, receded, and then closed into final, fibrous tissue I could live with. After those surgery years I was prepared when I cut my arm on window glass, when I delivered my daughter by C-section, when that same child fell on schoolyard ice and ripped her chin open wide. I had vitamin E and topical ointments, could determine from the set of each stitch how the mending was progressing inside. Scars, and the process that made them, were familiar presences, and I knew how to proceed in the face of them.

My father's scars, though, disarranged me completely. Not the surgical ones, those from his triple bypasses, his colon and wrist repairs, his plated-and-pinned broken leg, but those from his final great illness, when a doctor said his lungs were turning to scar tissue, that the scars were creeping like cracks in window glass, that they would not stop. They would not stop. They would not stop, the doctor said, and here my competence ended, my education failed, for I had never fathomed scarring as a disease in itself, as a malignant force to abhor. For all the sense it made to me at the time, that physician might as well have said night dreams were toxic; I would have been equally inadequate to take measures.

And the medical people, as kind—as ready to explain—as some of them were, could offer little by way of enlightenment. The very name of Dad's disease bespoke bafflement: idiopathic (meaning, "We don't know where this came from") pulmonary (meaning, "of the lungs") fibrosis (meaning, "progressive scar-ring"). Every journal article I read, every doctor with whom I spoke, employed verbal qualifiers every fourth word, saying *possible* causes of IPF *may* include inhaled particles of coal, asbestos, even dust; saying a certain medicine *might* calm the coughing and *some* people found *a degree* of relief in humidity; saying a patient *could* live for years in *relative* comfort *if* his disease halted progress, unpredictably, for a while. The amorphous half-concepts were difficult enough for me to grasp, and for my father—a Polish immigrant who spoke well but still needed me, oftentimes, to rephrase—they were well nigh impossible.

Also impossible, for Dad, was the notion that there was nothing in particular to be *done* about his illness, just a sort of "let's try this"—or this, or this—series of ineffectual cough suppressants, alongside ever-increasing dosages of bottled oxygen to convince his anxious lungs he was breathing. During boy-hood, Dad had survived Nazi internment because his own father had *done* things, made plans for escape, carried them out, led his sons hundreds of miles through wintertime woods, banishing gray wolves with his shout. Much later, in America, my father himself *did* things to get by, walked into car lots and offered to sweep for a couple of slim dollars or a meal. Times when he had no sleeping place, he asked for an overnight cot at the jail, promising to work at whatever they might give him in the morning. He met my mother, moved with her to Alaska, preserved our reclusive family by *doing* things, anything, so we could own land, could build a house upon it, could go out among trees unobserved. The efficacious, fervent prayers he'd mouthed those decades would serve him, also, now, but still he desired to *do,* to act, to take hold of his incapacity and prevail.

As, of course, did I. To be sure, I believed the books when they said this disease was a final one. I believed, too, that the hit-and-miss treatments would mostly miss, and that the number of possible therapies was small. I believed that no one understood these scars, their origins or design, and that even Dad's death date could not be predicted to the year. Even so, I could not— oh, Lord—wait passively, emptying his phlegmy wastebasket while he choked.

Thus, like my father and grandfather before me, I *did* hopeful, perseverant *things*—read texts (what few existed), researched drugs and vitamins, grasped about for knowledge. When my father asked, "Can you think why my skin is disintegrating," I telephoned around, found no answer, but fed him zinc and other minerals which the books said were beneficial to the flesh. When the drying rush of bottled air chapped his nose and throat, I ordered a humidifying attachment, looked into internal-use moisturizers, swabbed on whatever I found. For every symptom Dad suffered, I brought home a sack, set it down near his chair, and conjured out from it creams and capsules and any medical hardware I had found.

And oh, he was obedient, would try anything I told him

might help. After standard treatments ran out—the steroids having done nothing but made him "feel, um-m-m, *uncomfortable*" (he shifted his eyes toward me while informing the doctor, indicating, "I mean to say *sexual*, but my daughter's in the room."), the asthma inhalers having had no effect at all—we bought alcoholic liqueurs which he sipped, religious misgivings aside, from a small rounded glass, closing both eyes, drawing the vapors within. I said to sleep sitting up, to take in more and then less caffeine, to drink water, inhale steam, eat garlic or onions or cayenne, and each of these he performed like a child, nodding at whatever I spoke. Some measures, like the liquor, expanded his breathing for moments at a time, but none worked well or for very long, and by the end our house was a warehouse of half-full jars and bottles, greasy ointment pots, tried-and-discarded tubes, masks, and machines of every variety and cost.

By the end, too, he was tired, so tired that once he murmured, "For me, another Holocaust," meaning that here, again, were adversity and suffering, inhuman oppressors, an era of calamity when nothing a man did could preserve him. This was not, he would have said, his first annihilation, but it would— give praise—be his last.

In the years since my father died, I have seen photographs of scar-pervaded lung tissue. They are not so remarkably ugly, would cause no layperson to leap up in alarm. Lain side-by-side, however, with photos of healthy lungs, the images are clearly wrong somehow, the colors mottled, the texture more granular than elastic. Pondering these stark figures of infirmity, I profoundly apprehend Dad's affliction, and I wonder how it was he kept silence, broadcast as little anguish as he did. Days when long strands of scar broke free and came up his throat, lodging in his teeth like dental floss, he must have been in a panic, drawing in breath and feeling no more relief than if he'd inhaled tepid water from the kitchen. Toward the end of his illness—at the beginning, too, but more frequently later—Dad would say, "You'll miss me, of course, but remember to be thankful I am free." So this, now, is what I enjoy to imagine: My father among trees with a great wind blowing, the kind which expands a man's chest and fills him; I endow him with the broad muscles of his youth, fully oxygenated and strong, and I give him work digging postholes sometimes, or dragging firewood, even building a new house with his hammer. It strikes me as strange that I see him always thus, never sitting still or at rest; but however odd, the visions are forever active, my father industrious, his gestures magnanimous and brisk. In each of these dreams, he is singing.

# LEAH HAGER COHEN

If the side of your face lies upon a breast, then the top of your head nestles under a chin, and beneath your ear a heart beats. This is a place. The place may be hilly or flat, soft or hard, smooth or furred. It may smell of wool or milk, sweat or powder, cigarettes or soap or outdoors or oregano.

Men lay their heads on women's breasts; women lay their heads on men's. Children allow their heads to rest against the breasts of trusted adults. A man will not likely allow his head to rest against the breast of another man, nor a woman against another woman's, unless they are lovers, or the age difference very great.

In this place we fall asleep. We cry. We listen to a voice rich in the chest of the speaker, seasoned by the sounds of the speaker's own circulatory system, respiratory system, digestive tract. In this place we rise and fall. We speak quietly. We are comforted.

When I was very small, my father used to sing around the house a song, a spiritual, whose lyrics consisted mostly of the line *"Rock my soul in the bosom of Abraham."* For a long time then I thought "bosom" meant arms, not just any old dangling arms, but specifically crook-elbowed, cradling, sheltering arms. And well-biceped, besides—I didn't know who Abraham was, but surely he was male, and the image my mind created was of muscular, dark arms, protective and secure. A cool, welcomely detached embrace.

I don't remember under what circumstances I learned which part of the body "bosom" actually meant, but I do think by then I was already beginning to be embarrassed by the word. I know that by the time I entered first grade, I was aghast to learn that the librarian's name was Mrs. Breslow; I was mortified on her behalf. The word was embarrassing because the *things* were embarrassing, and the things were embarrassing because everybody wanted them, breasts, both sexes equally; they were desired, secretly, by all.

And what were they for, breasts? That much was clear: for boys to look at, of course. Oh, we knew about babies and milk and that, but we meant what they were *really* for, what they were mostly and most importantly for. The answer was readily apparent in the images around us on television, in department stores, in comics and cartoons, on our dolls, at our parents' parties, in shop windows, on cereal boxes. They were to decorate and be looked at. None of us had them back then, in grade school, but we could practice the idea of having them, try on what it might mean.

Part of that trying on meant parsing the lingo. New words for breasts came rapidly and abundantly. In third grade I learned a playground ditty that performed the mean feat of including what seemed to be every naughty word known to humankind in two staccato lines of verse. We chanted it, while waiting for the school bus, as if it were a mnemonic device for an upcoming quiz. Only one word had the distinction of appearing twice in the litany, first in the phrase "titty-sucker," and reprised as the subject of the second line: "Every time I look at you, my titties itch." To this day I don't know what *that's* supposed to mean, but it was an ugly word in any case, spat off the rough white edges of our newly acquired grown-up incisors.

But all breast words have a terrible sound. *Boob* is gassy and floppy and idiotic, as in "Ya dumb boob!" *Booby* is the same, but worse: cloying, infantalized, with the nyah-nyah echo of "booby prize."

*Tit* is hard and tiny and sharp; as a friend observes, it makes them sound like thumbtacks.

There's that whole list of words only boys use—*honkers, hooters, chachas, maracas, jugs, melons, sweater meat*—falsely celebratory, every one of them spiked with derision. Those words belong to imaginary breasts: the ludicrous ballpoint doodles of boys' spiral notebooks; the inflated, rigid orbs of men's wet-dream magazines.

*Bosom* is not so dreadful, I suppose, but it sounds antiquated to me now, high-necked and corseted (Abraham notwithstanding), bound up as a single unit: a vague, humped shelf draped in mauve, I think, or plum tweed. Eyeglasses on chains rest on bosoms.

*Breast* itself would be all right, only it's a little clinical, and a little crispy-sounding besides, with that chilly, officious double consonant at the attack and the arrested hiss which clips it off.

Another friend attempts to circumvent the whole semantic

dilemma by referring ironically to her "mammaries," which only underscores the problem: no good words.

We are named after breasts. Mammal comes from *mammalis,* as in mammary, or "of the breast"—meaning, in this case, exclusively that of the female. It is specifically the milk-producing glands for which we have been named, we as well as scores of other warm-blooded, hair-covered vertebrates. We have this in common: elephants and bears and warthogs and dogs and kangaroos and panthers and humans and mice. We have even been known to suckle each other, mammal to mammal, mouth to teat: piglet to woman, human baby to goat.

Our name comes from the shared event of milk, but we have invested the human breast with a quality regarded as unique to our species: we think of it as the seat of emotion. I suppose this is because it houses the heart. The breast, male or female, doubles as a kind of safebox against whose lining that vital organ beats, and since any strong emotion may cause the heart to race and thrum more distinctly against the breast, no wonder we have romanticized this spot. It's a mid-place, too, located a cerebral distance north of the genitals, a warm length south of the brain: the seat of ambiguity.

A random list of condoned behaviors: we clasp our breasts in horror, delight, patriotism. At conventions, we mill about with our names fixed upon our breasts. If we are handed a red carnation and a hat pin, we may wordlessly assume that the breast is their intended destination. A pendant may nestle between two breasts, as may a medal of honor, a lifeguard's whistle, a stethoscope, two hands in prayer. We do not, in public, cup the breast, wear a brooch or badge directly over the nipple, sport a flower between the two.

All of the male breast and great portions of the female are acceptable for viewing, including the entire upper swell and the dark gully in the middle. It's the female nipple, really, that constitutes the taboo. The nipple is the point at which the mild curve of suggestion stops and reality hits: biology, anatomy, floridity converge. The nipple ups the ante. It is brash, piquant, as unruly and aberrant as flamenco at a funeral, dew in a boardroom. The exposed female nipple has no place in public, no place in fashion, no place anywhere in fact but the bedroom, in private, under a lover's gaze or thumb or tongue. The nipple blows the whistle on the breast's true meaning and function, that being solely, at this moment in history, culturally speaking, erotic.

(The shared event of milk notwithstanding.)

I am small, and in that regard faulty, by the standard of the ballpoint doodle. By the standard of the ballpoint doodle all women are faulty, to varying degrees, which fact may be either imprisoning or liberating or both. I mean we may feel trapped inside our faulty frames, or free beyond the reach of such consideration. But the standard of the ballpoint doodle reigns, whether we care or no, so long as the breast's purpose is ornamental and erotic.

A woman's breast consists of fatty tissue and a mammary gland. The fatty tissue accounts for the erotic element; it's what makes breasts big, what makes them fill out lacy bras, and tight sweaters, and wet T-shirts; it's what makes cleavage. The mammary gland is the part that links us to other mammals, and has made it possible for the young of our own species to survive and grow all these millennia; it's what sustains us.

When I had a baby, imagine my surprise when I turned out to be a crackerjack nurser. I'd always thought of my breasts a little humbly, not to say apologetically, and even throughout my pregnancy, when I thought finally I'd acquire, you know, melons, maracas, the whole mock-gleeful chant, they changed little. It was with fond skepticism that I nursed my son in the hospital, and with true astonishment that a few days later I let them fill—amply—with milk.

And I—who'd always been what people refer to as "a slip of a girl"—took plain joy in my baby's fatness (eight and three-quarter pounds at birth, and consistently weighing in at the ninetieth percentile), knowing that every ounce of him came straight from my body. *I could feed a person.* It was a melody, a hymn, an ode to direct action. If his body was the genius for knowing what to do with it, mine was the enigma for conjuring the milk. It was conjured, really, what other way to put it? As a child I'd sort of gathered that cows alchemically turned grass into milk; now I was in that league, and what pure delight to see my milk metamorphose within his body into round wristlets, echoing chins, cheeks like ripe cheeses, a stomach like the moon. My milk made his tiny nails grow long; it made the drool that dripped from his curly lips; it made his eyelashes, which didn't appear for a few weeks. It even perfumed his dirty diapers; stools smell sweet on breast milk. What woman engaged in such a project could not love her body?

Very quickly, almost immediately, it came to seem like

something I'd been doing forever—not in the sense of boring, but in the sense of easy. I could nurse at the drop of a hat, anywhere, simultaneously with nearly anything. (It became a joke of my mother's to ask me, at absurd moments—while I was washing dishes, say, or showering—whether I was breast-feeding right then.) But I did, in fact, breast-feed while working on the computer, eating in a restaurant, stirring spaghetti sauce, answering the door. I could have my top undone in seconds, whether in pajamas or a cocktail dress. I nursed cross-legged in the grass, standing up at a parade, on a train, at the beach, in parking lots and offices and stores—once even as I traipsed through strangers' bedrooms and cellars, while house-hunting.

I might angle for privacy or not, as the situation seemed to warrant, but mostly I let my baby's appetite dictate the time and place for nursing. I reveled in the rightness of the action as much as in my own prowess, and cared not a whit for offending anyone; what could be less offensive than feeding one's child? But many people apparently confuse nursing with sex, and stories abound of women being harassed for nursing in public places. (The first laws protecting this action have come on the books only within the past five years; they clarify that breast-feeding does not constitute an "unnatural and lascivious act," or "lewd, lascivious or indecent conduct in the presence of a child," or "unlawful nudity or sexual contact," or "obscenity.") A couple of teenage boys once ogled me as I nursed in the backseat of a parked car. "Pretty baby," one ventured to comment, unpleasantly. "We need privacy," I snapped, outraged, *outraged,* at his sexualizing our activity.

Some women do report feeling sexually stimulated while

breast-feeding; I never did. Breast-feeding is, for me, a thing wholly apart from sexuality. It is cuddly and restful, satisfying and poignant, a form of primitive physical love, and a mutual, functional act of complete connectedness. When I wasn't simultaneously word processing or minding the stove, I would gaze down at my son suckling at my breast, and I have never drunk in such beauty. But none of this was to me sexy. And it was so clear and freeing to have my breasts divorced from the erotic; in a way it was the first time since grade school that my body had seemed uncomplicated, unconflicted—also unfaulty. I stopped breast-feeding him earlier than I would have liked to, at around five and a half months, only because I couldn't wait to get pregnant again.

With my breasts I poisoned my daughter.
"Never think that," admonished the nurse.
"But it was my milk that made her sick."
"It wasn't your milk; it was something *in* your milk."
"She was allergic to my milk."
"There's no such thing."
"It's what the doctor said."
"You must have misunderstood his accent."
"But he wrote it down for me."
I had it in his handwriting on a prescription pad, her condition in his surprisingly legible penmanship: *human-milk-induced colitis.*
She was born after just over an hour of active labor, and put immediately on my chest, in that place, the bosom, laid over my heart and held by my Abraham-arms. And then what

had torn on me was sewn up, and right after that she nursed; I nursed her; we nursed. And right away—she was perhaps thirty minutes old—she began to get sick, but we did not know that then.

Before she was a day old, she'd gained a reputation among the newborn nurses for having a particularly querulous cry. "Ooh, she's angry," they'd chuckle, popping their heads in the doorway. I didn't think so, but she did put me in mind of the Michael Ondaatje poem that begins, *Your voice sounds like a scorpion being pushed / through a glass tube.* At home we began to use phrases like "She sure is feisty," "She loves to be held," "She's no pushover."

It was five weeks before my husband persuaded me something was physically wrong. Actually, he didn't; it was only to humor him that I agreed to bring our daughter to a pediatric gastroenterologist. True, she cried—squalled—more than half of her waking hours, and true, it required great and lengthy feats of swishing and cradling and dipping—a kind of desperate pas de deux—to calm her down, and true, she did not nurse with the warm, blind contentment of her brother, who used to drink himself blissfully milk-drunk at every feeding. Instead, she would pull off my breast, and cry, and frantically bob her small head and latch on again, only to pull off. But it was nothing I couldn't fix, with my bosom if not my breasts; I'd clasp her there, in that place against my heart, and rock her around the midnight kitchen, softly, strongly, willing and dancing her into a tenuous rest-state.

The pediatric gastroenterologist tested her stool and found blood. Her colon was bleeding, most likely due to a protein allergy. He took me off dairy products, soy and soybean oil, eggs, and red meat. Ten days later, the crying had not changed and the bleeding had not stopped. We met the doctor at the hospital and watched him perform a flex sigmoidoscopy, inserting a tiny camera through our baby's rectum in order to view and take a biopsy of her colon. The tissue appeared bumpy, irritated, on the television monitor, and we could see tiny red lacerations here and there. *It's too bad,* said the doctor, nodding in agreement with himself, *but you'll have to stop breast-feeding,* and he sent us off with a free can of the special formula we were henceforth to use.

I cried in the car on the way home. We bought some bottles and found a store that carried the special formula. It hurt to stop breast-feeding all at once like that (with my son, I'd tapered off, to ease his emotional adjustment as well as my own physical soreness), but I expressed some milk in the shower, and took Sudafed to help dry up my supply, and it is almost true that I was too busy or addled to notice it anyway, what with an infant and a toddler and sleep deprivation and acres of spit-upy laundry and the like, and after a few days the soreness abated. And that is one end of the story.

Here is a postscript:

My breasts, as if sulking, went away. For a few weeks after I stopped nursing, I could still express a little milk if I tried, but then my body got wise and stopped production, and my breasts grew smaller, returning to their inactive state. But they didn't stop there.

My daughter's difficulties did not end when she started on formula, but persisted a few months more, through additional dietary tinkerings (for a while she got put on a special formula, imported from the U.K., that cost forty dollars a can), a couple of hospital stays, and various medications. During this time she continued to cry, furiously, many hours every day, and I lost my appetite and quite a lot of pounds. If before I'd been small, now I was gaunt. I had a washboard chest, withered and spent: a visual echo of my depleted sense of self, and as I struggled to mother I struggled, too, with my shrunken body. It disgusted me and reminded me of how I'd fallen short.

I knew intellectually it wasn't my fault, knew what that nurse had meant when she chided me for phrasing it so. But it was, after all, my breasts, my milk, that had triggered the allergic reaction that caused my daughter so much pain. And after everything we are told about breast milk being the very best, safest, almost preternaturally ideal food for our babies, it came as a terrible blow, my body's betrayal of my daughter and me.

For I mourned my own deprivation as well as hers, bitterly resented the loss of so many rich, peaceful hours of nursing. I missed establishing that fundamental connection with her, missed forming that perfect circuit of hunger and nourishment, need and fulfillment, call and response. Once, during one of her bouts of hysterical crying, I tried offering her my tiny, dry breast: if it could not give her milk, I thought at least it might offer her some calm (I'd heard that in some cultures a father will offer his nipple to comfort a baby until the mother returns), but she only screamed, and I added embarrassment to my despair.

When I had nursed my son, it was as if I were feasting, too, on a broth of well-being, as if I as well as he grew large in the process. In the absence of nursing my daughter, my whole self seemed reduced, inadequate. I failed doubly now: by the gaze of men and by the health of my child. To fail with one's body is so immutable, so absolute: a little preview of death. Privately, ashamedly, I mourned.

Another postscript:

My daughter is seven months old and robust. My son will soon be two. Yesterday the three of us were out on the grass, wrestling. Both children like to dive at me, openmouthed, locking their fingers in my hair and around my ears. They laugh and pant, openmouthed, against my cheeks and nose. It is a damp, heady business.

My daughter treats her bottles these days with a certain bored dismissiveness. She taps her fingernails against the plastic, picks at the bottle liner, pulls the nipple out of her mouth and regards it, chews it, bats it aside. She is more interested in actual food nowadays, gets a real gleam in her eye when she sees a banana, a burger, a leaf of chard; she's remarkably indiscriminate. For that matter, she will lunge with equal appetite at a section of the morning paper, a wallet full of credit cards, her brother's arm.

They are good cuddlers, both of them, and at the end of the day, like homing pigeons, invariably find their way back to that place: over my heart, under my chin, next to my breath, folded in my Abraham-arms. When I hold them here it is a place, nothing more and nothing less, and the only test is *do they tuck in warmly here, do their bodies fit?*

Occasionally they fall asleep, but more often they simply come to dwell and bask a little. In this place they rest their limbs. They lean, as if against a tree, and gaze with child-poise upon the world. Behind them, at this moment, I am the perfect shape. We are quiet in concert. My breath revolves within my breast; without, my children rise and fall.

# HANDS

---

## MONA SIMPSON

My image of the women I grew up with: they are sitting straight with a concentrated stillness, but their hands are always working.

Picking nutmeats out of shells, slowly filling clear glass jars.

Sewing hems by hand in tiny, even stitches.

Darning.

Filing and polishing each other's nails, on the kitchen table, using hand towels and custard cups filled with water and dish-washing detergent.

Combing children's hair, wetting a finger in a mouth to remove some piece of dirt from a child's face.

Even in leisure: shuffling cards, dealing, rolling dough.

In church, praying on rosaries. The nuns I knew were always fingering them. Priests merely let them sway off their cassocks.

*Never let anyone cut your cuticles, only push.*

This was imparted to me as if it had been carved on the stone tablets. God's own law. The implication: others will try to CUT. And once they're cut, I was warned, they'll never be the same.

(Incidentally, the same peril was ascribed to shaving; once

you shave your legs . . . the hair will grow back a different way.)

Girl children are presumed to have so many virginities.

*Always use gloves when you wash dishes.* Another primary commandment. Cream your hands every time after.

You can tell a woman's age from her neck and hands, I was told. Women will spend a fortune on their face, I was admonished, and then blow it all by scrimping on hand cream.

Preservation was a major tenet of a girl's education.

Even now, when people compliment parts of a child, her eyes or hands, I suspect them of grasping for something to say, as if there is an obstacle to the obvious exclamation. *What a beautiful child!*

I had the kind of hands that brought music to adult minds—piano or string instruments.

In another era or class or family, I might have learned needlework, knitting, embroidering, crochet.

But my mother was modern and artistically inclined, and so for years and years, I studied viola. I wanted cello, but when I started, at seven, I was too small, they decided, to hold the instrument between my legs. Mr. Hyman Weinstein was my teacher and I admired him, for he was a great musician.

I knew from the very few minutes—less than five total—he'd let himself play during my lesson. It would be at the end of some long frustration with me, when he'd finally allow himself to demonstrate a few bars. He'd lift the instrument to his shoulder with his chin—no hands—and then, eyes closing widely, his fingers would buss on the strings in strong vibrato.

Those were our best moments, his and mine. When the lesson stopped and he would let himself play music a moment. I closed my eyes and traveled at those times too. We both blinked back, refreshed.

Every time I wished he'd have let his hands go longer. But no. We were always back to me.

For all the years I took lessons, in a bleak part of town, the unremitting LA light against a dull stucco building, no color, the particular dusty yet iridescent green the trees seemed—I felt my teacher's disappointment. It was a regular presence in that room, a dim torso, near his downturned mouth.

Disappointment in me? No. In this whole worse world he'd found himself in, since the war. And in me a little, because he held the erroneous belief that I could be a real musician, like himself. He seemed to think I was deliberately preventing it.

"Let's take it again, from the third bar. This time with some feeling."

From another girl in the orchestra, I heard about hand insurance. Great pianists', harpists' hands were insured for millions of dollars. More likely it was really surgeons' hands. How marvelous, I thought, to have such value in your hands.

Some women in my family could make a perfect crust. It was a talent in the hands.

Some could do things with hair: braids, twists, parts.

No one's hands were insured for crusts or perfect stitches or tight braids.

In China, a kind of intricate embroidery, called Forbidden

Stitches, was outlawed in this century because the women who practiced this rare art went blind.

As early as summer camp, girls played endless hand games, slapping, clapping, *The Spades say, Tulips together, twilight forever, bring back my love to me*. . . . They rubbed each other's backs in canteen line and some people had talent in their hands, for touch.

Living in Los Angeles as a teenager, it was more than once suggested to my mother that I could pull in a good bundle hand modeling.

I'm not vain, except about my hands. There's a kind of certainty you get about something almost always remarked upon. You're kind of surprised if someone doesn't notice.

One of my students wrote, *Even the earth-mothers who wear Birkenstocks, start putting on makeup after forty*.

After thirty-five, most women revert to nail polish, I've noticed, what they loved at five and six and had no time for in college.

In Los Angeles, my mother's manicurist, a woman renowned because she can fix anything, drives a Mercedes.

This year, playing with four-year-old boys, I broke a finger. I went to the emergency room, then to a specialist, then to a hand therapist, who gently stroked the errant digit.

It is amazing how much one can't do with one broken finger.

I was told it would never be the same, which in my experience has meant the pain or recollection of the pain comes back, a blowing rag of fog, some days.

The finger feels arthritic when it rains, the way my liver echos its former hepatitis if I have a drink.

For the first time in adult life, my nails grew long enough to be pretty, because I couldn't use my hands.

The first poet I ever met was a middle-aged woman, a mother who told me she could read palms. I didn't much believe in such things but it made more sense than horoscopes. You use your hands so much. She said she'd read her husband's palm right before they were married and become very frightened. They were bad lines, all crossed over each other, with no order. She had been young and didn't trust her gift and they married anyway and had children. Years later, two plainclothes policemen knocked on their suburban front door and arrested him for embezzlement. He was in prison for six years. She took the children to visit, one at a time.

Now was already later, he was out, home, working as a mechanic. One Tuesday evening, she said, she'd picked up his right palm after supper and looked: it had completely cleared. Lines had straightened, simplified. What had crossed before was now parallel.

I wanted her to read my hand but I didn't ask. She also said she never read tragedy. She would put down a person's hand and say nothing.

★　　★　　★

On my own honeymoon, we stepped into a palm reader's office, on Martha's Vineyard. The outside placard promised a free consultation.

The couple before us outside slipped their wedding bands into their pockets and we did the same.

I don't remember what the woman told my husband. She told me something dire would happen in the next five years.

In Shakespeare's early tragedy, *Titus Andronicus,* when Lavinia is raped, the villain also cuts out her tongue and chops off her hands.

It's been more than five years now.

Nothing did happen.

What I do, write, I do by hand.

# Can't You Hear My Heart Beat?

## SHARON SLOAN FIFFER

"Your heart," said Sister DiBlasi, holding up her tightly balled fist, "is this big."

Each one of us, dutiful fifteen-year-olds sitting attentively in sophomore biology class, wadded up our own fists, stared and nodded. We wrote down our teacher's words in our notebooks and planned to answer the next day's quiz question correctly— the human heart corresponds in size to the human fist. But not all of us believed it.

It had to be bigger than that. I knew mine was. How else could it hold all my feelings, my passions, my desires, my dreams, my secrets? Oh sure, everyone knew I had loved John Lambert since eighth grade and Bill Ruder since September and John Lennon since the night I heard "If I Fell" on the radio and chose him as my favorite Beatle. But what about my secret love for Pat Grant, the coolest guy in our class who never said a word to me, and my dream of joining the Peace Corps before becoming a famous actress? I fell asleep at night composing my acceptance speeches for Tonys, Oscars and Emmys. I made space for them on my imaginary mantel next to my Nobel Peace Prize. I had a crush on a priest. I thought I could sing. I sneaked my father's cigarettes and practiced smoking them in front of a mirror. I planned ahead for my lapse of faith by skipping Mass regularly. Those were only a few of the secrets I kept locked in my heart. Those were the ordinary ones.

My father did have a heart bigger than his fist. Dr. Farlander told him so.

"You have an athlete's heart, Don, it's larger than normal size. Nothing to worry about," Doc said, lighting up a cigarette and cocking his feet up on his desk.

My father didn't like hearing that any body part was abnormal, but he shrugged it off. "Might as well have it be my heart," he said, when reporting the news of his physical at dinner that night.

"Have what be your heart?" I asked.

"The way I go, honey. I want a heart attack."

I didn't want to hear this, but my parents, like most, never talked because their children *wanted* to hear what they had to say.

"Yup, a heart attack's the way to go. It's fast. It's a surprise. Boom, it's over."

Several years after this conversation, my father's best friend, Milt Frechette, had a heart attack in the EZ Way Inn, my parents' tavern. Milt was playing pool, his cigarette burning in the ashtray, his glass of beer still cold on the bar. He sized up the table after the break, clutched his cue and collapsed. He was dead before the ambulance arrived. Boom. Surprise.

My dad went around in shock for several days. His face was gray, his eyes glassy. I badly wanted to ask him if he still wanted a heart attack, if he still wanted to go that way, just like Milt, while considering banking the number seven into the right corner pocket. I didn't have the heart.

When I was a small child, I fell asleep counting my heartbeats. I lay in bed trying very hard not to think about breathing, swallowing or the ka-thump, ka-thump, or was that a dreaded ka-thump-thump, marking time under my pajama top. If I could forget my body for a moment, I could sleep, but if my skin was particularly tingly or a soft buzz sounded in my head, I stayed alert, listening to the ebb and flow of my own blood. I thought this obsession of mine with breathing, with fearing my body would stop working if I yielded to sleep, made me unique, maybe even crazy, but in the adult exchange of childhood horror stories, I find that, as in most things, I am one of many.

One woman I know insists that as a child, she could track each bite of food as it moved through her system and that any time of day, she could tell you what part of her body held the cheeseburger she had consumed for lunch. My own Aunt Maxine told me that as a preschooler, she spent hours locked in the bathroom staring into her own open mouth, pulling out her tongue as far as she could, to see behind it, beyond it, to discover where her words were coming from.

Lying awake in my own craziness, clutching my teddy bear, Mortimer, I repeated over and over, Don't think about swallowing, don't think about swallowing, because, if I let up for a moment, I would no longer be able to automatically, unconsciously, swallow, breathe, maintain any kind of body rhythm. (As I write this, forty years after the height of my fear, my throat still constricts and I find myself gulping as I remember how loudly my heart beat, how grudgingly it pumped as I struggled before sleep.)

My mother, bless her own scarred and stony heart, was an overworked and unpaid partner at the EZ Way Inn, and had neither time nor patience for the illogical state of childhood.

"Just do it, just swallow. Stop thinking so much. Go to sleep," she'd call in from her room across the hall. My dad, pre-Milt Frechette's cardiac explosion, would already be snoring, at peace with his own large heart, sure of his own mortal choices.

Worse for me if my mother actually came in and had a conversation about my fears. "Well, so what if your heart stops beating in your sleep? You'd never know, so what's the difference?"

Comfort was not her forte.

I wish I could say that some great moment of enlightenment occurred that enabled me to put my childish fears aside, to understand my body and how it worked, to calm my nerves and give me peace. Instead, I just got older and started liking boys and listening to the radio and began thinking of my heart as the fragile vessel that held my hidden inner life.

So fragile, so filled with my unique joy and angst, that the wrong glance at the wrong time from the right boy could actually, literally to my way of thinking, break my heart. Swallowing, breathing, hah! They were nothing to the heartache, the bruised longing that translated to physical pain as I lay in bed, now with a princess phone and transistor radio instead of a stuffed bear squished beside me.

"He asked *her* to go *where?* Ohmigod, listen to what's playing, it was our song."

And as "Ferry 'Cross the Mersey" played into the night, my heart cracked crookedly through the middle. I wept in time to our song, one that I've since realized is a lyrical tribute to working-class life in Liverpool by none other than Gerry and the *Pacemakers*. Coincidence? I think not.

After eighth-grade romance, I entered Bishop MacNamara High School a sadder and wiser girl. In my head, I was ready for Sister DiBlasi and the hard facts of biology, but in my heart, that four-chambered vital organ only as big as my fist, I knew that what was being pumped through my system had to be more than blood. I saw those four chambers as the actual rooms where people I both loved and despised duked it out daily, fighting for my affection, my respect, my loyalty.

I still do. In that upstairs, left apartment, the people I loved and love still jostle each other for a seat on a folding chair to watch me muddle through my life. And everyone I blame for everything that went wrong, that still goes wrong, all those grudgees that still shouldn't have committed whatever against me, they sit there, too, on the floor of the right basement apartment. They get no chairs, no windows, but are simply on call for me to drag out and harass when I need to remind them that they did me wrong.

My father never got his heart attack. When the first surgeon general's warning about smoking was published, that gentle nudge that smoking *may* be hazardous, my father quit, cold turkey, just like that. He put on ten pounds though, and when he went in for his annual physical, his old-school, small-town doctor told him the weight would be worse for him than smoking. "Those extra pounds will be hard on your heart, Don," he cautioned, lighting up one of his own cigarettes at his desk. So my father went back to Tareytons, and instead of the heart attack that took Milt, Dad got the long, slow torture of lung cancer. Boom, surprise.

We can't make our bodies do what we want. We can train and strain and apologize for them, but they are what they are and they do what they will. In my twenties, I was on the verge of falling in love with someone. After a Halloween party at my apartment, intimacy seemed imminent. I was costumed as the Mousketeer Annette, and I felt that in all honesty, I had to reveal that he might be attracted to my costuming instead of the real me. I removed my long false eyelashes, my black curly wig and some padding. (Those readers old enough to remember Annette will know from where the padding was removed.) And in a burst of heartfelt honesty, I also confessed to him that I was a little overweight.

"Well, instead of first class, we'll just have to go parcel post," he said without blinking, and my heart opened up and he moved in.

We married and had a daughter and at twenty-eight, he died of ALS, a neuromuscular disease that his doctor assured us would affect neither his brain nor his heart. Right. Instead, it would affect mine. His breathing would be compromised, we were told, because the illness affected the voluntary muscles and "to almost everyone's surprise, the diaphragm is a voluntary muscle," his doctor said. Not to my surprise. I had known practically since I was born that breathing, swallowing and maintaining the rhythm of my heart took constant vigilance.

I fell in love again. My heart, perhaps as large as my father's, opened up for a wise, beautiful man who loved my daughter, Kate, as much as he loved me. He courted us both, and won us over. I gave him all the room left in my heart. I expanded the space when our daughter, Nora, was born and built on a new wing for our son, Rob, three years later. I was so filled up now, my heart, at times, felt like it might burst at the seams.

One night in particular, it seemed it would happen.

After Rob was born, I had trouble sleeping. Not too unusual. New baby in the house. Nora just beginning nursery school. Kate in double digits, taking on fifth grade at the middle school. Schedules, homework, lunches, play dates, groceries, work, life, what everyone has on her daily list. One night, I lay down next to Steve, both of us in the twilight exhaustion of babyworld, and as I heard his breathing grow more regular with sleep, mine became more ragged with waking. I wandered the house, watched the children sweetly inhale and exhale. Who had taught them to breathe so well? I returned to bed, repeating to myself, Don't think about swallowing, don't think about swallowing.

Gulping air, I listened to my heartbeats grow louder and louder. Ka-thump. They demanded attention. Ka-thump, thump. Irregular. An ache began in my chest and radiated down my left arm, just like the refrigerator magnet at my mother's house said it would if you were having a heart attack. My life was supposed to pass before me, but instead, I saw the future. No one would ever love my children and Steve enough if I were gone. Ka-thump, thump. I was too happy for this to happen. My hand tingled. What if my father's wish had stuck to me? Boom. Surprise.

I woke Steve and we argued about whether or not to go the emergency room. He was for, I was against. The more we debated, the calmer I felt. It wasn't getting worse. I promised to call the doctor in the morning. Rob woke up. I heard Kate talk in her sleep. Nora made a little noise when she turned over. All the rhythms of the house grew ragged, it seemed, so I could rest.

The doctor told me the next day that my chest and arm pain was "most probably" muscle spasms and aches. Maybe indigestion, too much caffeine. Nothing to worry about. I was balancing a baby awkwardly on my left side, I was out of shape, I was anxious.

Maybe. Or maybe I was just beginning to pay attention, the way I paid attention as a child. My heart tells stories. Every beat holds a love story, the overwhelming smothering wave I feel for my family, the sweet memory of every smile that quickened my pulse, the wistful farewells we begin composing when we recognize the lines in our parents' faces. Every beat tells a scary story, the what-if, the scenes of horror imagined and real, the nightly news of emotion that might happen to us, our family. Why them? Why not us? My heart beats in petty anger, too. Against every driver who doesn't understand the concept of the four-way stop, every teacher who didn't call on me, every child who hurt my child, and Jimmy who lived down the alley from me and ran over me with his bike, beep beep, fatso, here I come, then lied and laughed about it. My heart pounds thinking about it now.

Soft science about the heart? Maybe. Sister DiBlasi would be disappointed that I've become such a sentimentalist. But maybe we all just use different language and methods to figure out the same stories. Our bodies may equal mortality, but the tales they tell transcend, the stories are our link to immortality. Because I wanted to write about my heart, about listening to my heart, I feared the soft mush of emotion would permeate the page instead of the knife-edged prose I like to think I am capable of writing. Therefore, I turned to research. I consulted my 1966 eleventh edition *Merck Manual of Diagnosis and Therapy* purchased for one dollar at a garage sale. For hard science and crisp definition, I turned to the chapter entitled "Heart Sounds and Murmurs."

*Heart Sounds: The sounds, heard on the surface of the thorax, caused by vibrations associated with the successive events of the normal cardiac cycle. The origins of these vibrations may be valvular or muscular, or they may be due to motion of the heart or blood.*

The motion of the heart? Is that so different from what I've been saying? Oh, baby, baby, can't you hear my heart beat?

## The Fruit of Thy Wombs

---

## THOMAS LYNCH

The contemplation of the womb, like staring into the starlit heavens, fills me with images of Somethingness or Nothingness. It was ever thus. If space is the final frontier, the womb is the first one—that place where, to borrow Wallace Stevens' phrase, the idea of the thing becomes the thing itself. It is the tabernacle of our expectations. The safe haven we are ever longing to replicate in our latter-day habitats. A place where the temps are set, the rent is cheap, the food is good and we aren't bothered by telemarketers or the taxman. That space we are born out of, into this world, where the soft iambics of our mother's heart become the first sure verses of our being.

My mother taught me to say my prayers. I learned the "Hail Mary" in two languages, neither of which made any sense to me. I could sing it in Latin, angelic in my ignorance. But I said it over and over in English all through the days of my youth, encouraged first by my mother, then by the blue nuns who schooled me as a boy in the rubrics of Catholicism. It was where I first heard any mention of wombs. The rosary taught us to say them quick—fifty of them, with a sprinkling of "Our Father's" and "Glory Be's"—letting the words blur into glorious or sorrowful mysteries, Zen-like, a mantra for ritual mourning, family devotions, private meditations. But late at night I would linger over the syllables, pondering the imponderable meanings, and study the sense as well as the sound: "Blessed art thou amongst women and blessed is the fruit of thy womb Jesus." This struck me a strange benediction. Did Jesus have a womb? Was I missing a comma, a colon, a period?

It was early October, 1958. I was nine, about to be ten. Pope Pius XII was dying in Italy. I was listening to the radio and saying my rosary, staring out of the window into the night sky and wondering about wombs. The prayer observed the circumstances surrounding the birth of Jesus. It was first among the several stories we were taught by the nuns that had a decidedly sexual subtext. Here's what happened: a young Jewish woman, pledged in troth to a local carpenter, was minding her business, saying her prayers, when the Angel of the Lord appeared to her and gave out with the words that named this prayer, to wit: Hail Mary! Then, after the customary pleasantries, she was given to believe that she would soon find herself to be with child. This, she told the angel, was impossible as she and Joseph, good Jews that they were, had kept a cleanly distance in their courtship. Not to worry, says the angel, the Holy Ghost would impregnate her. No less a force than the Power of the Most High would overshadow her and the fruit of this union would be called the Son of God. This is Luke's version of it. Matthew reports a dream of Joseph's, Mary's cuckolded betrothed, who falls asleep much troubled by her apparent changes. An angel appears in his dream and explains that she hasn't been unfaithful—it was the Holy Spirit that filled her womb. *"C'est le Pigeon"* as James Joyce retells the French folktale in his great *Ulysses*—"It was the dove," the blessed virgin tells the carpenter. So here was the Remarkable Conception.

Then as now the church seemed to have an inordinate interest in the private lives and private parts of women. The high value placed on virginity was coincidental with an enthusiasm for fertility. That these seemed at cross-purposes was one of the several mysteries of a nunnish boyhood and my devoutly lapsed adulthood.

But I recall clearly that it was sometime in 1958, watching my mother grow large with the pregnancy that would become my sister Julie Ann, and praying the rosary for the dying pope that I began what would become a lifelong interest in the womb. There'd been five of us before Julie Ann and there'd be three more to follow before our folks were through, but it was the autumn of 1958, a year after the Russians launched *Sputniks I* and *II,* that the womb became the wonder of my world.

I'd seen an episode of *Playhouse 90*—a mid-century TV show—whilst spending the night at a friend's house, which portrayed the plight of unwed mothers. This formed in me the earliest curiosities about procreation. At ten I reckoned that marriage was the cause of pregnancy because folks got married and then had babies. That this seemed the natural order of things testifies to the protected environment in which I was reared. My mother was having babies all the years of my youth. Of nine of us, I was number two. The youngest of my siblings was born when I was sixteen by which time I had sorted out the relations between men and women and their babies.

It was after the *Playhouse 90* piece that I began asking questions of my mother about how someone got to be a mother without being wed. She spoke to me in her ordinary voice about love and desire, how God gave parents the pleasure of each other's company as a way of making babies, how it involved the dearest and nearest of embraces between my father and her and that someday I would meet someone I would love so much that I would want to hold her that way and that I would be a good husband and a good father to my children because I had what she called a good heart. She told me that this embrace, this intercourse, was so very pleasurable that men and women who loved one anther, loved to hold each other in just this way as often as they could. And the pleasure, she told me, was a gift from God given by nature as a kind of compensation for the duties and responsibilities of parenthood that inevitably and naturally followed. Children were precious and birth was a miracle and she and my father felt blessed to be part of God's plan. She held my face between her hands, she kissed me, she smiled, she returned to the ironing.

Then I asked Sister Jean Therese. I was twelve by now and I was admiring the breasts of girls in school and trying to figure out a way to get my hands on them and spending a lot of time alone in my room contemplating the mysteries of the universe and some magazines that Jimmy Schroeder and I found stashed in his basement under the stairs.

Sr. Jean Therese had wonderful breasts as well, though the black and blue habits of her order of nuns—the Immaculate Heart of Mary, IHMs—made every effort to hide them. She was very pleased I had asked her about these things and made no secret of that fact that the Facts of Life were better learned from her than from the boyos who hung out on the corner. And though I had never seen these fellows, and didn't know exactly which corner she was talking about, I made a mental note to search them out as soon as I was able. She explained to me in sensible detail the biology and physiology of reproduction, sexual attraction, the morality of the calling to married life. She articulated the proper names of parts and processes I'd never heard before. "Conjugal" and "uterus" and "semen" and "penis" were spoken with the same weighty precision as my mother had uttered "intercourse." She told me that men must assume responsibility for their behavior towards women. She said that sex was the most intimate language and that to speak such intimacies to someone we did not love was a little like speaking English to someone who only knew French. Eventually it would make no sense. Love, Sr. Jean Therese said, was the cipher, the code that made sex make sense. And sex, she said, was a gift of God to help true lovers understand each other. She carried on with metaphors and images, in hushed and breathless tones until, flush with what I figured was the Holy Ghost, she asked me if I had any questions. I was dumbstruck by the beauty of her breasts and intellections. She smiled warmly, much relieved, clearly pleased that she had passed this test with me. A holy woman in her twenties, a virgin bride of Christ, she pulled me to herself and hugged—my face buried deep in the space between her breasts, my cheek pressed against the heavy crucifix her order wore—I was not scarred for life but was, ever after that, a fool for love.

For his part, my father added to my tutelage thus. I'd gotten some glossy girlie mags from those boyos on the corner and made a pact with my brothers, Dan and Pat, to stash them in the attic space behind our bedroom walls. There they were discovered by my father during his weekly patrols. These were the years before children got quality time and their own space in exchange for their parents' time and interest in their lives. We assumed no right to privacy. He didn't trust our willingness to go to bed at night, our sudden interest in homework, the number of naps we claimed to be taking. He interrogated us as to their ownership. We all sang dumb, feigning wonder and innocence. He said he'd give them to our Uncle Pat who served in the local police department, to have the fingerprints lifted. If we wouldn't fess up, he'd get to the bottom of this. These were the days of Elliot Ness and the Untouchables and we brothers knew the long arm of the law could reach us. But we held our ground and worried for a week, then another. Dan got a rash, Pat turned insomniac, I thought maybe I ought to see a priest. When would the damning results come back from the lab? They never did. I only remember my father's forgiveness, albeit weeks later, fishing for bluegill on Orchard Lake, his quiet assurance that such curiosities, though normal, were better indulged in other ways. And his insistence that such magazines showed disrespect for our mother and sisters and would not be tolerated in his house. "Women are not just parts," he told us, "they are someone's daughters or sisters or mothers or wives."

So I owe to my mother and the nuns and my ever-vigilant father my earliest understandings, however biased and beautified they were, of the mysteries of life. They conspired to establish in my psyche indelibly the elemental connections between and among love and sex and nativity. These connections might be causal or correlated or coincidental. Folks might make love for the pleasure of sex, or have sex as a token of love, or have babies as emblems of love or as a consequence of sex. But these three things, love and sex and parenthood, were related. And the people who shared them were likewise related by blood or bliss or love or memory. More years later than I like to admit, the memorable pleasures of my clumsy first couplings were sharpened by the wariness I'd carried since watching *Playhouse 90,* that there might be some life-changing consequence of such behavior. It might leave us lovesick or disillusioned or with child. It might mean everything or nothing at all. But once touched by a lover with such approval, I knew I would never be the same.

Of course, the lessons of my experience, and the culture at large, include the ones that seek to disassociate those pieces of life's puzzle. Sex is frequently and fervently practiced absent love. "Free love" we called it in the sixties, as if by saying it could make it so. And babies are no longer the natural outcome of our couplings. More often they are reckoned a lapse in planning. Love or reproduction are less often the prime motives. On the contrary. Pleasure is preeminent. "If you can't be with the one you love, honey, love the one you're with." This was fairly easy duty. And, though it is true that I was passionately attached to my first sexual partners, and feel nothing but fondness towards them decades since, it was not love—I know it now, having known love since. We can, it turns out, disentangle the imbroglio of meaning and performance and outcomes. We can have love without sex, sex without love and both without babies, which we may acquire lovelessly and sexlessly in a lab.

We may, against my father's counsel, think of each other in terms of parts. And I often wonder whether I should count it a curse or a blessing that I came of age in an age when the reproductive choices of the species were expanding, just as their explorations of space were expanding. The personal was becoming politicized. We stared into outer space and reasoned there must be life. We stared into the womb and proclaimed it must be something else. Through the combined efforts of men and women, mankind has made it to the moon, but we see ourselves as creatures from different planets.

But just as outer space has been colonized, commercialized and politicized by late-century technologies, the womb, first among our species' inner spaces, has been likewise exposed, explored and exploited by invasive interests. So-called feminists, so-called Christians, so-called welfare reformers and social scientists all have staked their claim to the uses and abuses of its miracles. Bishops and abortionists—advocates on either side, true believers all—talk less and take sides more. Of all the existential questions asked of my generation, none has been more divisive than the ones about the womb—whose it is, what's in there, who gets to say what goes on with it. The borders of our reproductive lives have been blurred by a technology and a body politic that seems at odds. The starlit heavens have been easier to sort. Research may have dampened the romance, but by staring into space we have produced some global courtesies about space stations and star wars. Considering the larger universe, our national interests pale in favor of a larger citizenship. But the study of the womb, the arts and sciences of procreation, has disabused us of some precious mythologies. It has given us options more quickly than it has given us clues about the ethical, moral and practical implications. We are driven from the sweet expectant talk between parents and lovers into the polemics of planned parenthood and gender wars waged over life and choice, over the social, scientific, economic and political province of the womb.

To be pro-life one must be a radical Christian—a Republican or a papist or Baptist or a sexist brute who wants to impose one's personal morality on the culture at large, already suffering from patriarchy, and unwanted children, and abandoned welfare mothers and talk radio extremists. It's OK, the argument goes, for one to regard abortion as evil "for one's self," just don't try to limit everyone's choice.

To be pro-choice one must be a radical feminist, a left-leaning liberal, a godless social engineer working towards the dissolution of the family and of family values. Why worry about unborn whales if unborn humans are no more than "the products of conception." If the lives of the unborn, the pro-lifers argue, cannot be protected from the baby killers, who among us is ever safe?

I have a daughter and three sons. I'm in favor of Life, in favor of Choice. Life is not easy. Neither is Choice. My daughter and sons are biologically prepared and equipped for reproduction. Here are their choices as I see them. Each can choose whether or not, with whom and where, when and why, to be sexually active. They can choose how much or how little meaning it has, how much or how little of themselves to invest. Each can choose what, if any, precaution to take against disease and pregnancy. And should such precautions fail to protect—if they become diseased or impregnated, each has the choice to live with the implications or take their leaves. But if they choose to live, the available choices, up till now commensurate, take different directions according to gender lines.

My daughter, finding herself with an unplanned pregnancy, may choose to have the baby with or without the consent, cooperation or co-parenting of the fellow (shall we call him the father now?) who impregnated her. Or she may choose, in light of her life's circumstances, that a child would be terribly inconvenient and she may avail herself of what the courts have declared is her constitutionally guaranteed right to a safe and legal medical procedure that terminates her pregnancy, voids her maternity, aborts the viability of whatever it is inside her womb. No permission or approval is necessary beyond her willingness to exercise her choice. Whatever discomfort—moral or personal or maternal—she might feel does nothing to change the fact that she has acted within her constitutional rights. A pregnancy which resulted from bilateral consent is legally undone by unilateral choice. Our Bodies, OurSelves, the doctrine goes. If we uphold my daughter's choice in the matter we are said to be pro-Choice. If we consider the contents of her womb to have a life and interest of its own and that my daughter's choices end where those interests begin, we are said to be pro-Life. Either way, we get to choose which team we're on, which side we take, which sign to carry in the endless debate.

But if reproductive choice—the choice as to when one is ready, willing and able to parent—is a good thing, wouldn't it be good for my sons as well? And if that choice may be exercised after conception, as it currently is by women, then shouldn't men have the same option: to proclaim, legally and unilaterally, the end of their interest in the tissue or fetus or baby (depending on one's team affiliations) or whatever it is that sex between a man and a woman sometimes produces? As it stands now, paternity, once determined, means fiscal responsibility for eighteen years according to law. There is currently, for my sons, no choice in the matter. If they impregnate and the woman chooses to have the child, she has a legal claim against the income of the father. They may, of course, refuse to pay, refuse their paternity, in which case they are "deadbeat dads" or some other media-made phrase for "no good." But if their sister can choose, unilaterally, to void her maternity, and abort her parental role as a matter of constitutionally protected choice, why oughtn't my sons have an equivalent choice—say, within the first two trimesters, to declare their decision not to parent, to void their paternity, whatever the impregnated woman does, notwithstanding? Isn't this precisely the same choice given to women by *Roe v. Wade* and laws elsewhere that uphold this "right"?

But pregnancy and abortion, some several will argue, are women's issues, a woman's body. "It's none of your business," I am sometimes told. "Once men can get pregnant, then you can talk!" Is it really all about wombs, then? Is biology destiny, after all? As if condoms, the ones that fit on men's penises, are none of any woman's business. Or since only my sons are required to register with the Selective Service, their sister should be kept from the discussions of war, or foreign policy or defense spending. When someone is kept from the conversation because of their body parts shall we call it sexism or affirmative action?

Of course, the young men of my generation were quite willing to leave this a woman's issue. We had learned from our fathers and our mothers that babies—before, during and after their births—were mostly women's issues. The conventional image of expectant fatherhood involved a handful of cigars, a helpless vigil in a waiting room while the mother was in "labor." Then she would go home to her duties and he would leave home for his—his labor. Hers was to nurture and educate, his was to protect and pay. It was so for Lucy and Ricky, Ward and June. Father knew best and Mother stayed home with the babies. Young men died in wars, young women in childbirth. Old men died first. Old women died later, too often alone.

The division of labor was sane and sensible. The division of power, economic and political, of course, was not. Mid-century feminists identified the links between the womb and this imbalance. Tied to their children by a lifelong umbilicus, tied to their home fires by their indenture to the family, they could not travel light and fast like men who climbed the postwar corporate ladders, owned cars, wrote checks, ran the country. The oral contraceptive provided the first line of defense against the encumbrances of maternity. Abortion rights became the fail-safe. And the first waves of rapidly shifting gender politics that made landfall in the sixties and seventies instructed men of my generation that to question women on such issues would assure a lonely life. To get a little, in the parlance of our youth, we had to get along. Besides, we were only too willing to approve—sex without babies was a delightful concept. Freed from the

worry of pregnancy, women could relax and think about pleasure—ours and theirs. And pleasure, we found out, was portable
and modular. Love was nice but in a pinch, pleasure would do.
Talk turned to climax and clitorises, orgies and orgasms. G-spots
and casual, instead of causal, sex. The intimate lexicons of sex,
formerly meaningful because of their potential consequences,
seemed for a few years in the sixties and seventies "duty-free."
It was an illusion, but a sweet one.

And men of my generation were quite pleased to have the
dutiful business of reproductive life worked out in a deal struck
by earnest, rightfully angry women and lawyerly old men on
the Supreme Court. In 1973 the name given to this deal was
*Roe v. Wade.* Women saw it as freedom from the constraints
imposed by their wombs, their rightful ownership of their lives
and bodies. Men saw it as pretty much none of their business.

Still, if women wanted access to the office and factory, men
made their way into birthing rooms and nurseries. Inevitably
difficult questions arose.

Is it the species or the gender that reproduces? Aren't pregnancy and parenting human issues? I know they were when my
sons and daughter were "expected." Their mother was "ex-
pecting." So was I. And while a woman's body is certainly
involved in her maternity, a man's is involved in his paternity.
Women may choose legally to evict the fetus from their wombs
because their right to privacy includes dominion over their bodies and the bodies inside of them. But do we not ask men for
eighteen years of work and toil, their body's "labor" in support
of the baby born of their loins? If they refuse, which too many

do, we do not call it a privacy issue, we call them scoundrels. The former is optional, the latter is required by current law.

And though I am encouraged and inclined to march in favor of a woman's right to choose a safe, legal and affordable medical procedure to abort her maternity, where are the women who will march with me to uphold the rights of my sons and their sons in the matter—to choose a safe, legal and affordable legal procedure to terminate, for reasons that range from good to not so good, their paternity? Is Choice good for one and all or only one and half of the population?

"If they don't want the responsibility, they should keep their pants on!" is what I am told by several women of my acquaintance. Truth told, it sounds like sound advice. But the same advice, tendered to my daughter or to the daughters of my women friends, is regarded as suspect, sexist, patriarchal. "If you don't want the responsibility, you should keep your panties on." "You've made your bed, now lay in it!" "If you're going to dance, you've got to pay the piper."

"You just don't get it" is how it always ends.

Is it possible that the choices now legally available to women with regard to their reproductive lives, when considered for men seem irresponsible, overly indulgent, selfish and sexist and ultimately contrary to the best interests of the species?

What would it look like if a million men or so, next year, within twelve weeks of impregnating their sexual partners, were to declare, for reasons they had to articulate to no one, their interest in the fetus null and void, ceased and aborted? What if there were clinics, operated by Planned Parenthood, or a benign nonprofit, where the paperwork could be cleanly conducted for

a reasonable fee—these "procedures" done by lawyers instead
of doctors, assisted by paralegals instead of nurses, the deliver-
ance, safe, legal, constitutionally protected, the same for the fathers as for mothers? Would protesters march in front of such
clinics? Would signs appear calling them unflattering names?
Would pictures of destitute children, poor fetuses, abandoned
mothers punctuate these protests? If most of us are, as we are
frequently told, pro-choice, oughtn't the courts uphold this
choice as well?

In the past we have watched while the courts have decided
public policy on life and death. Policies designed to redress ex-
ceptional hardships have become the rule. An image we are
encouraged to conjure in defense of abortion rights is that of a
woman impregnated by rape or incest or at risk of her own life
by pregnancy, forced to line up in a back alley where some
heartless wretch has at her with a coat hanger. The image is not
a fiction. There are painful cases. People died. Something in the
system was very wrong.

Twenty-five years later we have abortion on demand, a million and a half of them every year, something less than five
percent of them performed on victims of rape or incest or
women at risk of their very lives. The other ninety-five percent,
presumably, occupy a place on the continuum between what
has been called a "life-affirming moral choice" and a bad decision. Either way: thirty-five million since '73; nearly one-third
of all pregnancies. There are few legal limits on when or why
or whom or how and any effort to moderate what has become
an "open season" is shouted down as a return to the back alley

and coat hanger. Many of those of us who favor choice, who uphold the individual's dominion over his or her body, now wonder if the present reality was the one we had in mind. Were there any other available options? To be pro-Choice must we tolerate all of the choices, even the wrong ones? To be pro-Life must we tolerate all of our lives? This is a difficult math to do.

The politics of the womb, like the politics of space, involve not only our public interests, but our private ones. And in the long-standing debates over the first frontier—who will be born and who willn't—the terrible din of public rhetoric has obscured the talk between fathers and daughters, mothers and sons, brothers and sisters, husbands and wives. We have been driven to the extremes, made noisome caricatures in a conflict which supports a growing industry of pollsters, politicos, lobbyists and pundits. The rhetoric of NOW defending late-term abortions sounds like nothing so much as the NRA defending our rights to AK-47s. Slippery slopers of different stripes, they fear the inch that will become the mile. They fear the reasoned, quiet talk between women and men, who see in each other's eyes neither creatures from Mars nor from Venus, but citizens of the same planet, fellow pilgrims, neighbors, lovers, teachers, willing friends.

Women are right to abhor decisions about their bodies that leave them out. So are men. The reproductive life of the species is not a woman's issue. It is a human one. It requires the voices of human beings.

One night before my first child was born, I lay in the bed beside his mother. She was sleeping. It was late November. We lived in a rented cottage beside a small lake. The night was dark, the stars were bright. In the half-light I could see her belly moving—hands or feet or head. I didn't know. But I knew what occupied her womb was partly me and would change our lives forever. Looking out into the night I spied the dominant winter constellation, Orion, and just to the right, the Pleiades— six of the seven sisters plain to see. To name a few out of the countless stars was a comfort. The woman sleeping, the baby bulging in her, the bright and blinking firmament alive, alive— I felt myself at ease on the edge of a new life, full of hope and wonder and thanks. I remember regretting that I would ever die. And remember knowing, for the first time, that I could.

## JANE SMILEY

### 1. VANITY

A week or so ago, I told my fifteen-year-old daughter that I thought I would get my navel pierced. This sort of thing is not unusual for women whose husbands have left them. A friend of mine saw his ex-wife for the first time in two years not long ago, and she (aged fifty-five) revealed that she had been doing a lot of surfing and snowboarding lately. When he exclaimed that in their thirty-five years of marriage, he had maybe seen her in a bathing suit twice, she shrugged heartlessly and went back to her book. A navel-piercing, I thought, would be just the sort of secret, sexy act to put me in the right mood for the last third of my life, which I plan to model on that of either Pamela Harriman or Victoria Woodhull—two independent women who seem to have crossed back and forth over the border between men and women with ease and without being taken captive by either side. A nice diamond stud in my navel, or the more classic gold loop, would be something I could reveal on selected occasions as a code for other soon to be revealed things about me that no one would suspect. My daughter was not at all charmed by the idea, either of revelations of my inner nature or of the piercing itself. In fact, she declared that me piercing my navel was both disgusting to think about and outdated, and she couldn't say which was worse.

The thing about the belly is that it is simultaneously the most real and the most abstract body part. It is a region rather than a spot on the map, rather like the Sargasso Sea is a region of the Atlantic Ocean that is defined but unbounded. The navel is the single little rocky island in the region. It would be nice to put a lighthouse on it, not to warn travelers away, but to give the region something to be or do. My particular belly region is about as small as it could be, which is the way I like it. I know that the real problem with the navel-piercing would be that I would do it only to show off, a bad motive if ever there was one. But even though the belly is only a region, it is one we are often obsessed with. Over the years, I have spent more time contemplating my belly than contemplating my face. After all, you need a mirror to contemplate your face, but you can look down any time and wonder what your belly is saying about you. My belly is my vanity—I never wear makeup and never do anything more to my hair than wash it and comb it, I think because as long as my belly is flat, everything is generally okay and I can forget the other stuff.

2. HUNGER

Right around the time I was pondering navel-piercing, a woman said to me, "Why are you so thin? You eat like a field hand!" It's true. I know how to shovel it in. When I was married to my first husband, who was six foot ten, I used to make recipes designed for six. He would eat enough for four. I would eat enough for two. Our ongoing conversation, which was the best thing about our marriage, always stopped completely when we sat down to eat, and we never dined for longer than ten minutes. We shoveled fast but we shoveled with pure pleasure. I also drink with gusto, big gulps of lemonade, Diet Coke, cranberry juice, water, whatever. Thus my life comes back, over and over, every day, to the belly, which harbors the stomach and the intestines. I know that appetite is in the mind, that taste is in the tongue, that hunger, perhaps, is in the gullet, but I am never quite satisfied until I feel that little stretch of the belly. James Fallows once wrote that Americans couldn't get enough to eat in Japan, because the food was fat-free; Americans, he felt, couldn't be satisfied without sensing that little smear of grease that lingers on the lips at the end of a good meal. I honor his opinion, but I don't share it. Volume is what I pay attention to, volume inside my belt. When there is no place left to put it, you have to take a rest.

Here are my favorite belly-fillers: French bread and French butter; eggplant parmesan; chicken cooked with saffron, garlic, and cream; chicken in a sweet red pepper sauce with Indian spices; jalapeno/artichoke dip with tortilla chips; sourdough toast; grilled ham and cheese; pork tamales; blue potatoes mashed with cream and butter. I like to cook and sing along to country music. If I find myself in a region of the country where it is difficult to find a good meal, I get impatient. Fortunately, I now live in California, where it is difficult not to find a good meal.

### 3. LOVE

Right around the time of the belly-piercing idea and the field-hand remark, I was sitting and talking to a friend of mine. I was recalling my first pregnancy, twenty years back, with a man now long ago and far away. I smiled, because that is what mothers do when they recall their first pregnancies. My friend laid his hand upon my flat belly with sudden and unconscious tenderness, the most loving gesture I have ever experienced.

Love, of course, shares the belly with hunger, and it is, from first to last, an uneasy association. Until pregnancy, the stomach and the womb are easily distinguishable. A gas pain is a gas pain is a gas pain, a cramp is a cramp is a cramp. No woman ever mixes up the two. But one little conception, and pretty soon the stomach has a lot of complaints to make. Particular foods are in demand—my last pregnancy featured a hankering, at all hours, for guacamole. Others called out for steak or buttered toast. Morning sickness was noon sickness and evening sickness, too. And then, as soon as that subsided, there was movement. At first it felt like bubbles popping, then it felt like fluttering from side to side, then it organized itself into kicks and punches and rollings-over. The bulbous shape of a little foot could be seen pushing against the now vast hump of the belly. The stomach and the womb talked back and forth to one another—whenever the stomach hurt, the womb responded with Braxton-Hicks contractions. Once I ate lobster and I thought the result would be premature birth. I gained forty pounds with one, forty-five with the other two. The stomach in its endless hunger expressed the needs of the womb, and the babies weighed in at eight, nine and ten pounds.

Even though I knew what pregnancy was, even though I knew the baby was not "coming" but was indeed here, active within, the vastness of the belly and the counterweight I developed behind dismayed me. No mirror or photograph could capture how large I was, no reassurance that I wasn't very big could convince me. My spreading pelvis and aching uterine ligaments told me that I wasn't well-designed for mammalian reproduction; no woman is. It's a miracle humans have survived as well as they have. I knew for a fact that pregnancy, and, say, hunting and gathering could not possibly go together. The only things that go together comfortably with the last month of pregnancy are floating in the bathtub and complaining. And that was before I brought my mind to bear upon the child's eventual mode of exit, which was one of those things that has to be experienced to be imagined, and even then seems impossible.

Oh the little horned womb, that fills up with love and then pings back into shape, leaving the belly once again looking bland and complacent.

## 4. ANIMALS

How fortunate we are to carry our bellies upright, the organs packed neatly, tightly, into the pelvis like items in a suitcase. Consider the Great Dane or the German shepherd, whose bellies have room, whose stomachs zig and zag, who, when leaping for a Frisbee, may feel a sudden twinge of pain that they don't understand and then die within hours of a torsion. My old Great Dane bloated twice, once after eating grass, which fermented in his stomach and locked the pyloric valve shut, so he couldn't throw up. Within twenty minutes of our noticing the first symptoms, he was going into shock, but he was immediately relieved, with a burp, when the vet put a tube down his throat. The second time was neither so easy nor so cheap. This time the stomach did turn halfway over, and required surgery. They tacked the stomach to the wall of the belly and cut away part of the valve into the small intestine so that nothing could get stuck in there ever again. And then there is the horse, ever and always in thrall to his digestive system. The horse evolved to eat vast quantities of poor forage fifteen to eighteen hours a day. The horse's belly is only really happy with a steady progress of greenery that never stops, never gets stuck, and never tries to back up. As they say in Pony Club, if your horse manages to regurgitate, he is about to die. The finest, best cared-for horse in the world can colic and pass on in an hour or two, the victim of a cascade of toxic effects that may grow out of a little belly pain. As with big dogs, the belly's position in the horse hinders rather than helps him. Once things get to sloshing around in that flexible space, they can turn over, get hung up, lose themselves. No matter how pregnant women ever get, they never, like mares, suffer from uterine torsion; gravity doesn't permit it.

Comparative anatomy is a trade-off—no mammal is quite right or quite wrong. Biomechanics giveth and it taketh away. Uprightness has given us back pain, on the one hand, but it has taken the pressure of gravity off our abdominal muscles.

## 5. STRENGTH

The last time I was in this post-marriage state, I studied modern dance with the eighteen-year-olds. Every day, we put on our leotards and our tights and began our instruction by turning out our feet, stacking our vertebrae, neck to tailbone, and then slowly and deliberately rolling our heads forward and down. We simultaneously dropped our pelvises and bent our knees. After suspending ourselves for a moment in the final downward position, we slowly and deliberately rolled ourselves upward again. The strength for this was all in the belly. It is the belly that protects and cares for the delicate spine. It is the belly out of which, in dance, all movement grows, until every dancer is the Indian god Shiva, balanced on one leg, arms spread in every direction, the other leg lifted high, energy flowing like light out of the mighty belly and spreading through the universe.

This time, I study horseback riding, which is quite like modern dance in its way. Once again, the belly is all, the center of the connection between the horse and the rider. Horses and riders are all backs—the horse's back muscles pass his strength and energy from his springing haunches to his supple shoulders and neck; the rider's back muscles flex and absorb the shock of the horse's movement as it moves upward from the rider's pelvic triangle to her shoulders, neck, and head. The rider's belly sustains and centers all this energy and prevents it from passing to her hands on the reins and locking there, against the horse's delicate mouth. Every day, the rider, like the dancer, puts her mind into her belly, and finds power there.

## 6. PAIN

My daughter reported to me that a girl she knew still has not recovered from her navel-piercing. Things seemed to be going well enough, with loose clothing and hip-hugging sweatpants, until the infection set in. Now it's been several months of agony, and she still can't wear a belt. I began at once to backpedal on my own navel-piercing fantasy. Perhaps a discreet tattoo would serve just as well, also on the belly, but at a distance from the navel and its nerve endings. The problem with a tattoo is that it has to be representational. A flower? How dull. A face? Whose? A name? Not erotic in the least. A butterfly or a dog? How like a bumper sticker. Actually, the only thing I can imagine that would be really fun to have tattooed onto your belly would be another navel, maybe with a picture of a diamond stud in it, and a line from Magritte underneath, *This is not a navel.*

# THE RESURRECTIONIST

## RICHARD McCANN

Here is what happened:

I was cut apart.

The liver of a dead person was placed inside me so I might live again.

This took twelve hours and thirty-three units of blood.

But who was I afterward?

I could still recall the body I'd had when I was ten, the body in which I carried what I called "myself," walking along the C & O Railroad tracks or crossing the divided highway that separated our house from the woods; a heavy, modest body, dressed in husky-size jeans from Monkey Ward and a brown corduroy car coat that my mother chose, identical to those my uncles wore back in the mining towns they lived in. I could recall the body I'd had, nervous and tentative, when I first made love at seventeen. But these bodies were gone, as was the body into which I'd been born; these bodies I'd called "mine" without hesitation, intact and separate and entire.

Six months after my liver transplant I flew to Nashville to visit my mother in the nursing home. She sat in a blue housecoat at a folding card table, slowly spooning a Dixie Cup of ice cream to her mouth. "Marie, your son's here," the nurse kept telling her. But my mother wouldn't look up except to look through me. She'd begun her own metamorphosis since the last time I'd seen her, withdrawing into the form of a bony old woman who only sometimes recognized my brother or me.

"Is this your son Richard?" the nurse asked, a grade school teacher prompting a forgetful pupil. My mother shook her head—*no, no.*

At night I sat at her bedside. "I'm here," I whispered as she slept. "I made it through. I'm here."

I didn't know if she could hear me. For a while I tried to work on the letter of gratitude I was planning to send to the strangers the transplant coordinator referred to as my "donor family," though I knew nothing about them or their loved one whose liver I'd received. I couldn't figure what to write to them that seemed neither too rehearsed nor too intimate, though I planned to repeat some remarks I'd heard in a support group meeting, thanking them for "the gift of life" and assuring them that the highest form of giving occurred, as theirs had, when neither the donor nor the recipient was known to one another.

For a moment my mother shifted beneath her blanket, murmuring in her sleep. I put down the pencil and closed my eyes. *In just a second,* I thought, *she'll say my name.*

"Mother," I said, though she said nothing further. I wanted us back as we had been, restored to what I felt were our real and original bodies, my mother smoking a cigarette on the stoop of our old house in Silver Spring and me beside her with a bottle of Pepsi in my hand, though I knew if my mother were able to ask what had happened to the liver I was born with—

the one she'd given me, I sometimes imagined, for it had once been a part of her as well as of me—I could have told her only what the surgeon had said: "It was sent to pathology and burned."

I flew home the next morning. On the plane I noticed the man beside me staring as one by one I swallowed the half-dozen immunosuppressants that kept my body from rejecting the organ it would forever perceive as foreign, and for a moment I felt my own sudden strangeness, even to myself, as if I were a distinct biological phenomenon, constructed in a manner different from that of my fellow passengers hurtling through space in a pressurized cabin, drinking coffee and reading their magazines.

"I'm a liver transplant recipient," I told my seatmate.

He wanted to know if my new liver was male or female or white or black.

I said I didn't know; he said that if it were him he'd sure want to find out.

But I didn't, or at least I didn't think so, and I was relieved when the plane began its descent. Somewhere over the Alleghenies my seatmate had asked if I'd heard about a man with AIDS who'd gotten a liver from a baboon.

No, I hadn't.

But in my transplant support group I had heard of recipients who'd waived their rights to anonymity to arrange what they sometimes called "reunions," inviting their donor families over for *Yahrzeit* rituals and barbecues, and I'd heard of donor families who'd secured the names of recipients, showing up unannounced on their doorsteps, bearing bouquets of mixed flowers and brightly colored Mylar balloons.

"Maybe it's kind of like discovering you're adopted or finding your birth mother," one woman said, confiding to our support group her anxious plans for meeting the mother of the teenaged boy whose lungs she'd received.

No one dared the obvious: the mother was the mother of a child who was dead, even if his lungs were still drawing breath on earth.

Sometimes I too fantasized that I had an alternate family that was eager to receive me as flesh and blood, especially as my mother retreated farther and farther into a world from which I was excluded, as when she imagined that I was her dead brother and called me by his name. But my fantasies of a happy meeting with a donor family were vague and unspecific, even less concrete than the fantasies I'd concocted as a child, waiting for George Maharis from *Route 66* to pull up to the house in his Corvette, ready to speed me away to what I felt sure was my real future.

My fantasies of a painful meeting, however, were explicit and detailed with dread. What would I say if my donor family were to ask to place their hands on my belly so they could feel the liver softly pulsing within?

How could I refuse them? I owed these people everything. I was alive because of a decision they'd made while standing in the bright fluorescence of a hospital corridor. Wasn't the liver more theirs than mine?

I imagined myself hesitating when they reached to touch me, and I imagined them demanding of me with what I would have agreed was a rightful anger, "Who do you think you are?"

★　　★　　★

We are made of the dust of old stars, our grade school teacher told us; we are made of leaves and sediment and the mulchings of life. But I was made also of something rescued from the graveyard, I realized after the transplant, and if I was now among the resurrected, I was also the resurrectionist—the name given in the nineteenth century to the grave robbers who sold corpses for dissection to physicians and anatomists, trafficking in bodies and parts.

I don't recall when I began to think of what is called "the non-heart-beating cadaver donor" as neither a noble but faceless benefactor nor as a nonhuman organ source, but rather as someone particular and separate who'd lived his own life before he died. I don't recall when I began to think of a donor organ as a bearer of its own set of cellular memories and not just as some sort of bloodied and perishable apparatus that one could airlift a great distance in an Igloo cooler marked HUMAN HEART or HUMAN EYES. In the eleven months I spent waiting for a transplant, I could barely acknowledge what was happening to my own body as my liver rapidly failed: Abdomen grossly distended from accumulated fluids; muscle wasting from my body cannibalizing itself for nutrients and proteins; pale stools streaked with bile; profound and constant exhaustion; brief spells of aphasia; cramps and sudden hemorrhages, blood puddling in my mouth from ruptured esophageal varices; skin the color of copper and eyes the color of urine.

I do recall a spring afternoon a month before my transplant, when I was lying on the grass in Rock Creek Park, back from the transplant clinic where I'd overheard a nurse telling someone in the next room—I couldn't see who—that a high number of teen-aged donors die not from car wrecks but from suicide.

I didn't want to know this, not as I myself was growing so desperate for a donor. As soon as I left the clinic, I asked a taxi driver to take me to Rock Creek Park—"Are you all right?" he kept asking, afraid of my appearance—where I'd often gone when I was well to sunbathe with my friends, though now I was alone. I paid the fare; then I was lying on the unmowed grass, attempting to lose myself in the song I could hear playing on a far-off radio, pretending that my whole life consisted of just one word: *Sunny, sunny. . . .*

But it didn't work. My donor had begun to claim me, or so it seemed; I felt as if he'd somehow been constructing himself inside me without my knowledge as I was dying, though he was still alive and waiting for nothing unforeseen. Perhaps he's here right now in this park, I thought, or perhaps he's in another part of the city, crossing a street against traffic or standing at a pay phone or waiting for the bus that will bear him home from work. For a moment it seemed as if there were but the two of us left in the world, me and my blood brother, though one of us would soon be dying.

*Don't die,* I wanted to whisper, though I didn't know if I was speaking to him or me.

I suppose I found out four weeks later: the hospital paged me past midnight to say they'd located a suitable donor.

My friend Sarah drove me to the E.R. The whole way I kept checking and re-checking the contents of the small suitcase I'd packed six months before—silk dressing gown, twenty dollar bill, packet of Dentyne, razor and toothbrush and comb; I couldn't stop touching these things, as if they were all that was left that was holding me to earth.

I knew what would happen when I got to the hospital—X ray, EKG, and enema; introduction of IV lines, one in the left hand and another beneath the collarbone, for sedatives and cyclosporine and antibiotics. For months, I'd been trying to prepare myself for the transplant surgery, studying the booklets the doctor had given me, one with drawings of abdomens marked with dotted lines to represent incision sites, and another with a diagram showing how a pump-driven external system of plastic tubing would route my blood outside my body during the time when I would have no liver.

I was prepared to wake in the ICU, as in fact I did, unable to speak or move, brain buzzing like high voltage from prednisone. But I was not prepared for what came the week after that: the impact of the realization that I had participated in the pain and violence and grief of a human death. *You have to face what you've done,* I kept telling myself as each day I watched myself in the mirror growing healthier, until even my jaundiced eyes were white again: I had taken a liver from a brain-dead corpse that had been maintained on a ventilator during the removal of its organs, so that it looked like a regular surgical patient, prepped and draped, with an anesthesiologist standing by its head to monitor blood pressure and maintain homeostasis, its chest visibly rising and falling with regulated breath.

"It's not like you killed him," my friends kept telling me.

"I know, I know," I said to quiet them, though I didn't know, not really, except I knew, as perhaps my friends did not, that it wasn't just children who believed they could kill with the power of a thought or a word. After all, I had sat in the clinic waiting room with other transplant candidates, joking that we should take a rifle up to the roof to shoot some people whose organs we might like. "I wish we'd been at the Texas Book Depository with Oswald," one man had said.

At night in bed I often thought of the person who'd died; when I was quiet, I could feel myself quietly grieving him, just as I was grieving my own body, so deeply wounded and cut apart, though still alive.

"I'm sorry," I wanted to tell him.

Sometimes I woke in the middle of the night, troubled to realize that I had taken a piece of him inside me, as if I had eaten him to stay alive. When this happened I often forced myself to think of it longer, though I didn't want to, as if I were a member of a tribe I'd read about a long time before in an old ethnographic text that described how the bereaved dripped the bodily fluids of the dead into their rice, which they then made themselves eat as an act of reverence and love.

In this state, I could not console myself. I got up and sat on the sofa. *So here I am,* I thought, *right on the edge of the unspeakable* . . .

Other nights I thought of the donor with a great tenderness, sometimes perceiving him as male and sometimes as female. These nights, I placed my hand over what seemed to be still her liver, not mine, and slowly massaged the right side of my body—a broken reliquary, with a piece of flesh inside—all the way from my hip to the bottom of my rib cage. "It's okay, it's okay," I whispered over and over, as if I were attempting to quiet a troubled spirit not my own.

*If I could, I would undo what I have done,* I thought, though I knew that if I had to, I would do it again.

I wasn't new to survivor guilt. After all, I'd been living for a long time in the midst of the AIDS epidemic while so many of my close friends died: Larry, Ed, Darnell, Allen, Ricardo, Paul, George, Arcadio, Jaime, Wally, Billy, Victor, and David.

In this sense, it had been a relief to be diagnosed, to have a progressive disease that threatened my life, to be bivouacked with the others. "It's like you're one of us now," my friend Kenny had told me. "It's like you've got AIDS."

But I couldn't tell him it wasn't true, at least not after the transplant; it wasn't the same at all. I'd outlived everyone, even myself.

What did Lazarus want after he stumbled from the cave, tied hand and foot with graveclothes, his face bound about with a napkin? *Loose him,* Jesus said, *and let him go.*

I survived. It's two years since the transplant. Here I am, in my new life.

I want to unfurl.

I want to become my gratitude.

I want to fly around the world.

I want to be a man with a suntan. The man in the Arrow shirt.

And above all, this: I want to complete what I've written here—these fragments, these sticky residues of trauma—by adding just one more line before the words THE END: "It's a miracle."

It is a miracle, of course. I know that. Just the other day, for instance, stopping at a sidewalk fruit stand and buying a blood orange: *Oh,* I thought, *this will replace the blood I lost.* I carried the orange to the park where I sat in the sun, lazily devouring its juicy flesh, its piercing wine-red tartness. *There's nothing more than this I need,* I thought. *I'm alive. I'm alive.*

But what happens after the miracle? What happens after the blinding light of change withdraws and the things of the earth resume their shadows?

What happened to Lazarus after his resurrection? On this, the Gospel According to St. John is silent. Did Lazarus speak after he was commanded from the grave and his shroud was unloosed? Did he thank the One who was his Savior and then walk back into the house with his sisters Mary and Martha so they could wash him clean? Or did he turn in anger toward his Savior, demanding to know why He had tarried so long with His Apostles before coming? *If thou hadst been here, I had not died.*

Where did he go afterward? Did he live a long life? Did he forget his time in the grave?

Here is where I went after my resurrection: Miami Beach, Sarasota, Raleigh, Nashville, Peterborough, Madrid, Barcelona, New York City, and Provincetown.

And I went back as an inpatient to the hospital—five more times, at least to date. The hepatitis goes on, the doctor tells me. The transplant doesn't cure it. It gives the virus a new liver to infect and feast upon. *(Dear donor, forgive me, I can't save your life. . . .)*

A year after the transplant, just after the anniversary the social worker called my "first birthday," these things happened: low-grade fever, weight gain, edema; jaundice; sudden and unwanted elevations in alkaline phosphatase, bilirubin, and liver enzymes. *This can't be happening,* I thought, *not again.*

"We need to biopsy the liver," the doctor said. He said we needed to measure the progression of the disease by assessing the extent of new cirrhotic scarring. I knew what that meant: It meant the story wasn't over, as I so badly wanted it to be. It meant that things were uncertain.

"Don't worry," the doctor said as he sorted through my file. "We can always discuss retransplantation."

No, I thought, I can't hear that word, not ever again, especially if it's applied to me. Where was the miracle now? I was supposed to have been restored. I was supposed to have been made whole. I wanted to unloose the graveclothes; I wanted to unbind the napkin from my face; I wanted to be through with death forever.

Instead I was sitting in a windowless medical office, waiting for the phlebotomist to come and draw more blood. I wasn't sure I had the heart for more miracles.

Did Lazarus believe he was done with death after his resurrection? There's no record of whether Christ cured him of the sickness that had killed him in the first place, before he rose again; there's no record of the pain his body must have felt after having lain four days in its grave—long enough to have begun to decompose and (as the Gospel says) *to stinketh.*

As for me: for three weeks I got worse; then I slowly got better. A few months later the doctor said there'd be no need to discuss retransplantation, at least not yet, at least not in the immediate future.

It wasn't a miracle that pulled me back, at least not then: I was saved not by a sudden and divine intervention but by the persistent and real efforts of physicians, some with Cartier watches and others wearing scuffed shoes. The story didn't end with a tongue of flame or a blinding light: each morning and evening I monitor myself for organ rejection, as I'll do for the rest of my life: blood pressure, temperature, weight. I go to the clinic for blood draws; I await faxes detailing test results.

Here is what happens after the resurrection:

Your body hurts, because it's hard to come to life again after lying so long in a grave, but you set goals and you labor to meet them, holding yourself up with your IV pole as you shuffle down the hospital corridor, slowly building back your strength. You learn your medications; you learn to pack your wounds with sterile gauze; you learn to piss into a bottle and shit into a pan. It's work, preparing yourself for sunlight.

Then the day comes when you are allowed to wash your hair and shower. A little while later you're walking down a street.

People you've not seen in ages stop to ask how you're doing; you say you're doing fine, you're doing great. It's life again, dear ordinary life!—life as you hungered for it, with its pleasures and its requirements.

Yes, it's life again, *your* life, but it's not the same, not quite, or so it seems, because you can't forget how it felt to lie in the close darkness of that grave; you can't forget the acrid smell of the earth or the stink of the moldering graveclothes, especially now that you know, as you never did before, that you're headed back to the grave again, as is everyone, and you know this with a clarity you cherish and despise.

The gift of life is saturated with the gift of death.

Sometimes at night alone in my apartment I imagine I am back in the hospital the night of my transplantation. I am sitting naked on a bed in a small cubicle behind a curtain, waiting for the nurse to come and prep me for surgery. *This is what it feels like to sit in a cold room,* I tell myself, because this might be my last night on earth and I want to feel everything, to feel once more how life feels, each breath in and each breath out.

The nurse comes in and tells me to lie on my side so she can administer an enema. *This is how it feels to be filled with warm water.* I go to the toilet. Afterward I look at myself for a moment in the mirror before I return to the bed so the nurse can shave the hair from my abdomen, all the way from my groin to my chest. "I hope my hands are warm enough," she says as she spreads the shaving soap across my stomach. She touches the cold razor lightly to my belly, and I think, *This is how it feels to be alive.*

# A Note on the Dink

## RON CARLSON

It would be exciting, if in writing about the most openly celebrated and reviled body part I could shatter a few myths and create a few others, but we all know already that it is the center of so much of the world's mythologies, the source of all major and minor religions, the focus and motor of all marketing, in fact the basis of capitalism (to which it gave its name) and every nonsocial economy, the name and nickname of every rock group and many musical chorales, the true axis of planet earth in this solar system, the hinge that opens the door to understanding, the axle in the big wheel of desire and regret, the bolt that keeps the door to understanding forever sealed, the first radical pillar of society, and the lone last digit of the secret combination on the lock of heaven, so I am going to have to settle for a few minor remarks about the penis, which like nuclear power has been best described as mankind's most potent friend *and* foe.

### MARVIN'S QUESTION

The relationship between a man and his private parts is never serene; there is always an element of intrigue, mystery, open conflict in the mix. For years, of course, having a penis is an absolute convenience. You get nine, ten, eleven great years of simple and efficient water work out of the thing, and the lesson it has for boys is clear: point that thing out there. It does not engender introspection, inspection, circumspection, or any other form of spection. You're busy chasing insects, small animals, your sister; riding your bike, the swings, the whirligig in the park; throwing balls, rocks, small animals; climbing fences, the garage roof, trees; playing tag, baseball, war; and, when you feel the need, you locate your penis and point it away and urinate. It is so straightforward an activity that you don't give it a second thought. That's what is necessary to know about the way men are trained: they are not practiced in second thinking. You're ten years old hiding in a bush and in a twilight game of tag, and you have to piss so you unzip there quietly as the kid who is IT approaches. Get it over with, because you're going to have to run for your life in ten seconds. It's what you do.

Then it starts to get unnerving. In the spring of sixth grade, the girls at Edison Elementary are all called into the auditorium to see a film with their mothers. The boys are kept in Mr. Durrant's room and not told one word about the whole deal, except it's clear from the looks on everyone's faces that the world as we knew it is coming to an end. And we boys knew it well, we had mastered this world in fact, liked it, loved it really, and it was over. They were complicating it. Nothing would ever be the same.

This moment is the moment that will give all future conspiracy theories a chance. Something's going on.

Mr. Durrant sits with the sixth grade boys in his classroom, and we visit informally and have a talk where he deflects all our questions with phrases full of "hygiene" and maturity." He throws around a few mystery phrases, among them *genitals*. I don't care. I sit there in the blond afternoon light of Mr. Durrant's classroom and wait for the bell to ring. The clock is ticking on our childhoods, but there are still forts to be built, rocks waiting to be hurled. I'm not listening to any of this; it might go away.

But it doesn't. At the corner of Concord Street after school, Marvin Hilbar stops me. "Hey, Ronnie," he says. "What's going on?" I tell him I don't know. Behind him I can see all the girls and their mothers drifting out of the school in pairs towards their cars. They all look down, serious and brave, as if burdened with some new grief. They walk away as from some state funeral. It is too surreal and then Marvin goes on. "What's going on with Durrant?" he asks me.

"What do you mean, Marvin?"

"What's this *genitals?* He said *genitals*. We've been going along all this time and now we've got *genitals?*" Marvin Hilbar's face bears a look I've never seen before, the kind of worry that will engender and fill volumes of self-help books for the next forty years, and he says, "I heard Mr. Durrant say *genitals*. How many you got? Because I just got the one." And for a real minute there on a corner that is as real a place for me as any in my memory, I too felt the little twinge of worry. It hadn't hit me sooner, because I was in denial. We were at that place where we crossed over and now it would be other people giving our bodies words. *Genitals?* Get out of my way. We didn't want any. We wanted to be boys.

So, childhood ends on that corner. We've still got all the gear, Little League, bicycles, trees—but everybody knows, even without being able to say it, that our old world is lit with a different light. It was a garden, lush and carefree, and then the girls see a movie and we're all asked to pack up and get out.

## THE SECOND PURPOSE

Then the rest of the news descends. The second purpose of the penis makes itself manifest. It's been behaving strangely for years, changing shape of its own accord, standing for who knows what reason, getting many times right in the way. We understand only part of this, that is, we know it is possible to cause the phenomenon. But other times the phenomenon arrives unannounced, an open surprise, like a spaceship full of hormones landing on the front lawn; where is it from and who sent it? And is it friendly?

And the language! We never, *ever* use the word genitals. Ye gods, scrotum, a word that could easily make the finals for most ungainly, unlovely body word, is easier to say than genitals, because scrotum is unscrutable, but genitals has that blatant Latin root which could link us with fatherhood in a hearty synapse. Meanwhile we use everything but Latin roots to name this male member; in fact, I've heard it called "the latin root" (a prep school joke), and it has the honor of having more nicknames than any other facet of the human body. Listing them here would be ten thousand words, if not eleven, and they've been catalogued elsewhere already. We started with dink and prick and weenie, but *never*—in our neighborhood—peepee. We had dong and tallywacker; schlong and wanger. There are quiet, but real connotative differences between single- and multiple-syllable words, and as any man will tell you, there are times when it has more than one syllable. There are names which accurately describe it as something like a goofy and benign gadget, and those that make it seem like an uncontrollable and savage weapon. There are pet names, ridiculous names, people's names. What all the nicknames speak to louder than anything is the sense of dichotomy that this appendage creates in the hearts of men.

I've heard it called Little Davey, Dick, and Johnson, as well as unit, member, thing (and of course, thingie). If we were really looking at the penis, its form and function, in the body, it might more often be called Che and Fidel, because there it is, standing at the crossroads of the body politic, in the center of town where all roads converge, stopping traffic and waving its flag, and when it stands the rest of your quiet little town listens. Your body may have had perfectly logical and well-measured plans for the day and now there's this uprising, and not way back on the wrong side of the tracks at the edge of town, this is the first thing about you; when you walk into a room, it goes first.

The human penis, of course, is a fleshy member containing no bones or cartilage. The walrus penis has a bone in it, an evolutionary device called the "oozik" which is a great help in cold water. The human penis becomes erect when engorged by blood, and the blood it takes to inflate the male member is exactly the amount of blood needed in the portion of the brain used for conscientious behavior. You cannot, as some of the vernacular goes, *think with it,* but it can certainly detour and delay and rewire what you should have been thinking.

The cause-effect feature of erections has all been rewritten by impotence studies, most recently the general release of drugs including the now famous Viagra, which makes it necessary for women to ask, "Are you happy to see me or is that your prescription in your pocket?" Viagra and all its stimulating cousins are fine; their availability should be based, however, on doctor's orders, a waiting period, and a background check.


## RETURNING THE SPELLING TESTS

Nocturnal emissions, many times, are most young men's first experience with ejaculation. They make you realize, even more than the random unbidden erections of boyhood, that life in a male body is going to be, some of it, beyond your managing. You go to sleep during a period of your life when your cells are screaming and singing with growth. Sleep, though you resist it, is like nectar. And you wake up having committed something. Evidently Little Willy has decided to act in your behalf, and he and his sidekicks have gone out and struck in the night. You sit on the edge of the bed and check out this little mess, viscous and confusing and daunting, and then the dream emerges through the mist: you talking to Veronica LaMonge, speaking to her beautiful face, a girl who sits three desks ahead of you and one over in social studies, a girl so ideal you've never spoken to her in person or touched her hand when she passed back the spelling tests (or made eye contact), and in the dream you are talking to her, explaining how you raised the handlebars on your bicycle and painted it yourself, speaking real close to her face, in fact so close that your arms are around her and you can feel the warmth of her breasts, and feel the pressure of them, their very curves against you, curves you've only seen indented against the ledge of her old school desk, and then your hands are in her back pockets, her healthy bottom, pulling her without compunction or worry directly against the hot place where Fidel stands beaming, waving his flags and shouting his raw and inflammatory exhortations, commencing once and for the revolution. Of course, the moment fuses, and there's an explosion.

## LOCATION, LOCATION, LOCATION

About this same time in a young man's development, the location of the male appendage becomes a source of comfort and anguish. It's right there within easy reach, an incredible design advantage. If it were closer to the knee, masturbation might be more of a challenge. But not much. Masturbation has been celebrated as self-abuse, entertainment, and hygienic physical relief. In case young men were slow to catch on, the penis is put right in front of everything, and when the hand falls at arm's length, the fingers naturally curl, and it is this length of arm and curve of hand that helps tailors cut suit sleeves perfectly and every man to find his little revolutionary.

We've been told day and night for years to keep our hands to ourselves, and now finally that seems like a good idea. It is, for the untutored, which is exactly the condition of every incipient masturbator, a remarkable activity. So clever and stimulating, with such clear results!

I remember having first stumbled across that frontier and being certain in my guilty heart that I had invented something dire. My junior high team was playing a Saturday morning game at the National Guard Armory on Sunnyside Avenue and in the big cold empty room as I ran the hardwood floors I have a vivid recollection of the couple dozen people in the room, parents and siblings and coaches and the two pale skinny teams, and I was worried about them all. The tide had risen for me the night before, and I had sought and found its release (one of sixteen thousand ways to say that phrase and not be too indelicate), and I felt—at twelve years old in the seventh grade—if I could find a way to tell them all about this thing that was happening to me, which I had certainly created, they too could have knowledge. It was a burden. I know that for three or four weeks that strange year I was the least innocent person on this round world.

## QUANTITY

As an athlete, as a boy during these years, I showered with the other boys on the team or in my class, and in passing came to see a hundred or two other penises, pale or dark, long and loose and small and tight. I didn't worry about it too much because such activity was normal and there seemed to be a fine variety of penises and I was sure that mine, which had been such an interesting and engaging part of my own body, would measure well—neither last nor first—in the pantheon of penises. Comparison seemed irrelevant.

In the pamphlet left on my bureau by my mother, the drawing of the male organ in profile did resemble mine, sort of. It actually looked a lot more like Florida, the capital of which is Tallahassee.

Size, does it matter? Bigger is better; less is more. The rule of thumb (a nice phrase in itself) became size doesn't matter. It was what you did with what you had, the sexperts told us. It didn't matter, they said, whether you carried a pen or a peninsula. The reality for a man is simply that when the penis grows erect it is in the way, which is another way of saying, plenty. The sperm whale's penis when erect is nearly fifteen feet tall; the grizzly bear, most closely related to man, has erections that average four inches in length, and require more cooperation from his mate. This size thing has generated its own macho mythology, the way that any concealed weapon might. Most recently the old phrase "size doesn't matter" has been given a new life in American marketing by a new generation of boors. It was (and will remain) a gauche thing to say anywhere but a doctor's office, and it announces again a focus on the wrong side of the issue.

Size matter, of course, but not in the obvious way. When the penis first does its little parlor trick, standing at attention if not parade rest, of course it is arresting. That the penis could grow alert enough to transform into the rigid single-minded agent of sperm delivery, every orgasm containing enough male gametes to populate six of the seven continents, is a wonder that handily eclipses the other side of this phenomenon. But when size matters is through the regular days of regular guys, those moments, hours, days, weeks, months which make up the 99 percent of our lives when the riot of sex subsides and the smoke has cleared and the citizens have gone to their homes or work and we're walking around not tall, but small. Size matters most frequently to every man in that his penis can shrink, adjust, do everything but disappear, retracting like the head of the sage—and long-lived—turtle. We're not talking normal here, but smaller. This isn't flaccid, another word that has been utterly appropriated for the male organ. This is much tighter than that. The testicles go north and the penis itself buttons itself up against the abdomen. It wants one thing now: to be out of the way. This is a fabulous design feature, but not one men are quick to note or illustrate. It becomes effective and necessary however when we run a marathon, ride a horse, spring cross a tennis court to slice a backhand winner, change a tire, sit perfectly still in that chair in the boss' office going over our expense accounts with the boss himself and the comptroller, or wake suddenly to the ringing phone at quarter past three in the morning. We are not however going to read the scene where a man celebrates how small his little penis was able to become at a moment when he needed it to be tiny, just really tiny. "I was so small, man, it was just amazing!"

## BALLS

There's an obligatory moment in every recent American film where the good guy kicks the bad guy in the groin. It's a square shot and has the bad guy doubled up in a second, both hands cupped over what we actually called the *family jewels*. He can't breathe. His eyes are crossed. He goes down. It's a kind of coup de grace in stupid film fighting, and I, for one, have seen enough of it. The testicles, part of the plural of genitals, have a near perfect design, as the scrotum is wired to hold them tight or let them float. When someone actually kicks you in the balls, as the testicles are called from here to Provo, most often—but not always—they slide off the blow, with the same motion that makes bobbing for apples a viable sport. In my neighborhood we walked the top bar of the steel fences, and I became a champion at it, able to tightrope along for a hundred yards. There was no one more surprised than I when my tennis shoes slipped one day and I fell to a sharp straddle on the steel bar. My buddies froze, anticipating the groan, the gasp, the fall, but not this time: my tender testicles, sensing first contact with the metal, rose softly up and let my bottom take the blow, and I dismounted intact and, after a moment's inspection, with a smile.

I wasn't always so lucky. I took a couple of direct hits. The worst was in the batter's box when I was fourteen, during an Automotive League baseball game. Every pitcher knows the way to brush a batter back is to throw inside, the way to hit him surely is to throw behind him. You know the batter will instinctively twist back right into it. I don't know why this kid wanted to hit me, but I know he did, for he threw a sidearm fastball behind me and I turned in the half second I had and took the pitch as solidly in the balls as any blow I've ever received. On the ground in a second I curled up and waited. The pain from such an injury is not unlike a sharp ice-cream headache (in the abdomen just below the navel) in that when the first wave hits you know there'll be five more large rolling swells that work toward a kind of crescendo and then only gradually subside. That day, after a minute looking up into my coach's face, I took first base under my own power, standing shakily in the strange new day. A moment later, after they'd retired the side, I stood in the outfield and the tremors of pain continued large and regular and then as the sun tilted, I swooned, crashing into the grass, the only time I ever fainted in my life. Centerfield was lush and green and probably the best place a boy could choose to go over like a door.

The left testicle, of course, hangs lower than the right because of the epididymis, that sperm-keeping curiosity, one of a very few things that spoil the symmetry of the male body. When you get fitted for a new suit, the tailor always asks which way you dress, meaning which side of the inseam does your member fall. Left: it's always left.

## THE REAL GIRL

O.K., so I've tried to say this and that. I haven't even tried to imply why all the great wise men of old (and of new) have founded all the religions of the world on their own sacred and delicious and confusing relationship with their own penises. Some of these members are thousands of years old. No great religion has ever been founded and sustained by a woman. That's all you need to know. None. The penis has got us all under its spell. *Scrotum* and *flaccid* and *engorged* may be off the mark, but *potent* is right on target.

Where I am is: at seventeen years old I had made an uneasy truce with my own penis, a bright pretty thing which I washed every other time I wasn't pulling at it for a reason that rose from deeper in me than reason. I suffered and benefited from the soft chronic schizophrenia which is the natural state of living in a body.

I met a girl. For every boy there are two girls: the ones you know pretty well because they are featured in your fantasies, and though you only know them in photographs there is some posture or expression that has become for you a sweet single ticket for release. Your wild Fidel rises, needs to really, and with a little manipulation and the right spread in *Playboy,* he speaks his piece. This is just physical.

The other girl is something else; the other girl is a real girl, and she embodies the quandary that is at the center of so much of our literature. She complicates everything wonderfully with a notion we sometimes call love. When I was seventeen I sat in the window of a Mexican restaurant in deep downtown Salt Lake City with such a girl. This was near Exchange Place in the shadows of the old office buildings, their gray facades ornate and metropolitan in a city with so few glimpses of urban note, and the restaurant, which has been gone so long now that it feels like something I'm making up, which I am not, but that's too how it felt to us then: that this was simply a set arranged so we could transcend the ordinary errands of a school day. There was honestly a red-checked tablecloth and we sat there like what we were, that is, young people about to enter the world. It was like being lost in our city for that moment, and I noted her smile and her auburn hair, and I had a faint sense even then that I was in, that this was it for me. I'm setting this all down because there I was with a member—as the saying goes—of the opposite sex, thirty months away from bringing any sex into the equation, and when we did begin the exploration and adventure of sex, there was my old friend, the penis, but things were different for us now. He wasn't the first guy through the door. I was first and he followed. It makes sense to separate us this way. He'd had his way with me from time to time and would again at the odd moment, but now the penis played only his supporting role. I was in love and wouldn't get out. I was happy for all of it; and these thirty years since it has been my life. The lesson ends here. The oldest lesson. You think you know the pains and pleasure of living in a body and then love doubles everything and then doubles that again. The penis makes sense at last.

After having been pushed and pulled and rent in twain at times, fires in the streets of my heart, people running in panic through the alleyways, breaking glass, sounding alarms, suddenly there was a quiet and the street lamps came on and people came to their porches to listen for music which also arose, and the revolution had done its work, found its reason, important alliances had been formed, and in the new vigorous peace, there was a discussion, a banquet of new proportion, and then dancing.

## CHRIS OFFUTT

My happiest memory from childhood is riding a bicycle in eastern Kentucky, raising a cloud of dust on dirt roads and following footpaths through the woods. For the first time, I could outrun the grown-up world. Nothing mattered except the pure joy of motion. I was free.

At age ten, it seemed natural to pedal furiously down the road that led off my homehill to the creek below. Halfway down I wrecked. My left knee swelled and my mother took me to the town doctor, who said I'd pulled a ligament. The bike wreck was typical of my childhood. I was always cut, bruised, bleeding, or walking with a limp.

Now I am forty and living in Missoula, Montana. A few days ago, I removed the training wheels from my youngest son's bicycle. James is five. He straddled the tiny bike and rode along the sidewalk with tremendous pride. Half an hour later he was riding his older brother's bicycle. I realized that Sam, who is a second grader, was also ready for a bigger bike. I visited a few shops, and came home with two new bicycles.

My wife Rita was gone with the kids, and I placed the bikes in a dramatic fashion, with helmets hanging from the handlebars.

My sons would see them upon their return. I sat and stared at the bicycles gleaming in the mountain light of spring. They were beautiful machines ready to propel my children away from me. There would be wrecks and crying. There would be glory and freedom. It is said that people never forget how to ride a bike. That is not true of walking.

At age nineteen I left Kentucky and hitchhiked to New York City to be an actor. After one horrendous audition, I embarked upon an alternate career as a piano mover because I knew how to drive a truck, a marketable skill in Manhattan. A month later, I hurt my left knee playing football in Riverside Park. The following day I limped to a hospital. My knee was swollen and unable to bend. The doctor said I had severed the anterior cruciate ligament, and recommended immediate surgery. Scared, hurt, and far from home, I refused the surgery, a decision I regretted for years.

The ACL is the strongest of two ligaments that holds the leg bones together. Without it, my lower leg was no longer anchored to my body. With a sufficient degree of stress, the thighbone and shinbone would disengage from their proper positions beneath the kneecap. It hurt like the dickens. Putting it back hurt much more. Learning to do so occurred while I was busy with a young woman in college. Unfortunately she misinterpreted my howl of pain as sudden increased desire, and my leg flopped askew for far too long. Afterwards I realized that my knee had popped in and out of joint. I spent a week on crutches, and another week limping.

For the following eighteen years, I guarded my wounded leg with the tenacity of a mountain lion. I stopped playing basketball, football, and softball. My leg was unable to tolerate the quick pivots of sports. I formed the habit of standing with my weight on the good leg, facing the world at a slight angle.

During the 1980s I held part-time jobs, living without insurance, car, or telephone. I walked everywhere. My employment was labor that kept my body moving. The knee stayed together, held in place by muscles that were strong from work. By decade's end, it was no longer a source of pain or sorrow. I was thirty, I was married, I had a trick knee. I told myself that considering my lifestyle, a bad leg was lucky. Many of my friends were dead.

During the next few years, I sat in various small rooms, writing for many hours a day. I gained weight. The muscles of my leg became soft. My chief activity was walking in the woods, usually alone and off-trail. I worried that a fall might jerk my knee apart, and I'd be trapped in the woods. I began hiking with a hatchet and rope, and even practiced making a crutch from a sapling. At thirty-eight years old, a husband and father, I was engaging life with the constant possibility of losing my ability to walk. It was a shameful secret. The knee embarrassed me the same way acne had as a teenager.

In 1996, financial desperation brought our family to Albuquerque for a one-semester job as a visiting writer at the University of New Mexico. We arrived in January, eager to begin anew. With any luck, the job would evolve to full-time and we'd remain there. After years of moving, Rita and I were ready for permanence. Our family needed security.

My sons played soccer and baseball, undertook lessons in piano and akido. In the evenings we played board games. Sometimes we wrestled on a king-size bed. In order to end a wrestling match, I usually allowed the boys to shove me off the bed, thereby granting them the win. In May of 1997, I rolled off the bed and my knee popped out of joint for the first time in many years. I lay on the floor amid the waves of familiar pain. I yelled for Rita and told the kids not to touch me. They felt terrible, their small faces in despair. The youngest was crying. Prone and unable to move, I told my children it wasn't their fault, that my leg had always been weak, and that I had let them push me off the bed.

After a week on rented crutches, the leg failed to improve, and my wife made an appointment with the hospital. X rays were inconclusive. The doctor sent me to a specialist with a machine that measured the resistance of the ligament. A dozen people were in my group, all athletes younger than I, all limping. After more tests my diagnosis was lousy.

The ligament was not only severed, but my body had long ago absorbed the stubs, preventing any hope of reattachment. A rubbery tissue, called the miniscus, separates the leg bones at the knee. It acts as a gasket, preventing the ends of the leg bones from scraping each other. Twenty years of repeated injury to the knee had shredded the miniscus. The bones were now surrounded by tatters. When I fell off the bed, one of these tatters had lodged between the femur and tibia, beneath the kneecap. In order to walk, I needed surgery.

The doctor told me that a torn ACL was the most common sports injury. Orthopedics, he gleefully explained, was the only branch of medicine that used power tools. He wanted to install a new ACL. He could graft one from my body, or use a ligament from a cadaver. Using my own was more invasive, but cadaver parts carried a risk of infection, particularly AIDS.

Several years ago I managed the Ninth Avenue Thrift Shop in Manhattan, a store that catered to transvestites in need of large shoes, and junkies looking for a place to nod off. I have spent many hours in used bookstores. Every car I've ever owned was secondhand, and most of my clothes. The only rule was no used underwear or socks, a rule I now extended to body parts. I chose a graft.

The problem was that I had no insurance. People urged me to claim that I'd gotten hurt on campus, which would force the university to pay the medical bills. Regrettably, I refused to lie. Though we lived in a good area, ten minutes' walk to the university, our house was burglarized. Three months after taking a job to improve our lives, I was broke, robbed, and crippled. I felt like a failure as husband and father.

Shortly thereafter, the Guggenheim Foundation gave me a grant based on a project proposal which entailed traveling to Alaska. I called the foundation, explained my injury, and asked if they wanted the money back. The director said that I should use the money for the operation. I thanked him, and a week later Rita drove me to the hospital for surgery. We were terrified but determined. I undressed and removed my wedding ring for the first time in ten years. A nurse helped me onto a gurney. An anesthesiologist administered morphine, which felt as if a sledgehammer had struck me in the chest. I remember reminding the surgeon to work on the left knee. I remember laughing.

While I was unconscious, the surgical team opened my leg

and cut a strip of ligament from the patella, which is the tissue that covers the kneecap. The chief surgeon drilled a hole in the end of my femur and tibia. He inserted the graft into the holes, screwed it to the interior walls of the bone, and stitched everything together. Essentially, he had restrung my knee like a tennis racket.

I awoke groggy and in pain, lying on a hospital bed. My left foot was strapped into a machine that slowly pumped my leg, forcing the knee to flex and straighten. Attached to my arm was an I.V. connected to a morphine drip with a timed controller. Every three minutes I could squeeze a hit of morphine into my veins. The drug was like a wall that had been built to contain the pain, a wall that instantly began to crumble, and after three minutes had collapsed. As the wall came down, the pain increased. The last thirty seconds were unbearably slow. The next day I went home in order to avoid the charge of fifteen hundred dollars per night.

For a week I took Percocet then went through three days of withdrawal. I was unable to walk, bathe, or prepare my own meals. It is impossible to carry a cup of coffee while on crutches. I was as dependent upon Rita as a child. The worst aspect was the humiliation I felt before my sons. They'd forever know their father as a weak man who required assistance with the most mundane events. In the afternoons, I hobbled to the porch and watched them ride bicycles with training wheels. Be careful, I called to them. Watch out. Go slow.

To avoid further expense, my physical therapist gave me a set of exercises for home. I spent three hours per day working my leg and another hour riding a stationery bike. The rest of the time I wore a heavy brace that ran from ankle to thigh. A month after surgery, I graduated to a smaller brace and a cane. In addition to my exercise regimen, I took long daily walks along Route 66, which runs through the center of Albuquerque. I came to know the shopkeepers in whose stores I rested. On the street I watched drug deals occur and tricks being turned. I witnessed an armed robbery. I heard gunfire in daylight. People offered an amazing array of illegal goods to buy.

After a few weeks, the therapist made me walk unaided. The muscles had atrophied. My knee hurt terribly as I limped in front of the therapist. She told me that limping was habit. Though my knee was now repaired, I'd spent half my life favoring it. My therapist observed me carefully. Pick up your heel, she said. Match the stride of one leg with the other. Let your arms swing naturally. Above all, she stressed, don't limp.

Most of us have been walking so long that it requires no conscious thought. We simply move from the refrigerator to the table. We go from our house to the car. Learning to walk again was the most humbling experience I've ever known.

Our neighborhood was good, but someone broke the window of our car and removed the stereo. Our house was robbed again, this time while we were at home, and my boys began to fear bad guys entering our house at night. Gang-type graffiti appeared in the area. When our car was totalled, we learned that Albuquerque led the nation in car wrecks. During all of this, I continued to walk. Don't limp, I told myself, don't limp, don't limp.

A year later, with leg intact, I left New Mexico. The climate was superb, but the neighborhood was becoming more and more violent. Our children could not ride their bicycles without constant supervision, which meant they could not ride their bikes. We could have moved within the city, but the University salary was not enough to support our family. We were disappointed to leave. Once again, the family was rootless, hoping to find a home.

We moved to Missoula where I took a one-year position as visiting writer at the University of Montana. We had rented our last three houses over the phone, and had arrived with a U-Haul and lots of hope. The same pattern repeated in Missoula. A year passed and the job ended. The landlord wanted to sell the house at a price we could never afford. I applied for a tenured position at the University of Montana, but the job went to a local writer whose sister was the director of the creative writing program. Our future was unsure.

I felt as if I was unable to provide stability for my children. I worried constantly about money. Buying new bicycles was a giant expense. I sat in the garage looking at them, hoping their purchase wasn't a mistake. I had no idea where we would live next. The uncertainty was crushing.

Rita came home in the same car that was wrecked in Albuquerque. The faces of my sons seemed to glow when they saw the bicycles. They knew instantly whose bike was whose, and they raced away in a matter of seconds. Their voices were pitched high with excitement as they thanked me, a sound that I savored when it echoed in the garage. Rita left the car and hugged me.

The horrible summer of pain and rehab, the monstrous medical bills, the terrible isolation in a strange town—none of it mattered now. My knee worked. I could ride my bike with my sons. They were coming back from the corner, their expressions intent with glee and power. They looked at me because it was important that they saw me watching them. I wanted to tell them to slow down. I wanted to warn them to be careful. I wanted to protect them like I had guarded my knee for half my life. Instead, I grinned as they rode past.

Go, I yelled. Go, go, go!

## KYOKO MORI

I never saw a ghost when I was growing up, but if I had, I would immediately have known that she was not a living person. A ghost would have long tangled hair, eyes wide open with sorrow or half-lidded in accusation, fingers like melting tallow, and her white kimono would be worn with the left collar over the right—the reverse of how a living woman would wear hers. But the most telling feature—the definitive mark—was this: a ghost had no feet. Almost any living person, after a great illness or suffering, might be afflicted with a vacant stare, pale waxy skin, and tangled black hair like grief itself, but only a ghost was doomed to float a few inches above the ground for eternity, her legs ending at the ankles. She could never again touch the earth with her feet no matter how desperately she longed to return to the world of the living. That was her punishment for failing to accept her death with perfect resignation. She should have been happy to float up to heaven to sit in a cloud of peace and beauty with her ancestors; instead, she remained hovering over the earth she loved, trapped by her undue desire.

I grew up in Japan, where my Buddhist grandmother told me stories meant to teach me to respect my ancestors, to cultivate a sense of resignation and quiet wisdom, but I wasn't the kind of child who learned the right lesson from the right story. What she said about ghosts did not make me want to live my life in such a way that I could leave it any time without undue regret or attachment. The story made me love my feet because they were what made me a living person instead of a ghost. On the summer afternoons my mother, brother, and I spent in our grandparents' village in the country, I walked on the riverbank, letting my toes sink into the warm sand. Where the sand was wet and cool, my feet left deep imprints. I admired the long row of perfect footprints trailing behind me. At six or seven, I already had the strong, wide feet of a long-distance walker and runner. In the river, I practiced the breaststroke—bending my knees, flicking my ankles, kicking out, then in. My feet were like propellers pushing me forward under water. There was no doubt about it: I loved my feet.

When we were not visiting my grandparents in the country, my family lived in Kobe, a port town. My mother and I spent our Saturday afternoons going shopping, visiting museums, getting our hair done, stopping for lunch or tea. My grandmother's Buddhist wisdom and Japanese food seemed as far away as the long train ride it took us to get to her village. Most women I knew in Kobe, including my mother, wore boxy-shirt-and-short-jacket outfits in light blue, creamy yellow, or leaf green with moderately heeled shoes in beige, navy, black. They were sensible good clothes and shoes, attractive but practical. Many women my age, who grew up in the sixties in middle-class families all over the world, must have had mothers who dressed the same way. Our mothers' clothes and shoes were comfortable and pleasantly—but not threateningly—pretty. They were not the plain work clothes of women on farms; nor were they the tight-fitting bodices, short skirts, and spiked heels of the women we saw in movies.

The shoes I wore as a child and the attitude I was encouraged to develop about my body were reflections of my mother's sense of what was comfortable, appropriate, and pretty. I wore sneakers and rain boots to walk up the long hill to the grade school my brother and I attended. My shoes had to be wide and flat so they would not pinch my toes or rub my heels raw, but they were not the plain white sneakers and black boots my brother and other boys wore. My sneakers were all different colors. Every year during the rainy season, my mother bought me a new raincoat and matching rain boots. I also had dress shoes: several pairs of Mary Janes with rounded toes and adjustable buckles; my favorite pair was red patent leather. By the time I was in the third grade, I knew what my favorite colors were: red, pink, purple, black—never yellow, orange, green, or brown. To understand which colors went together and didn't, all I had to do was to picture my favorite dresses and shoes. This was how I differed from boys: I knew about colors and I wasn't embarrassed by my knowledge.

Sometime during grade school, I must have heard about how Chinese court ladies used to have their feet bound because the noblemen prized their small, white feet the size of teacups. Undoubtedly, every time my family turned on the TV, I must have seen beautiful women—both Japanese and Western—walking awkwardly in spiked heels or trying to run away from danger and falling down because of their beautiful and useless shoes. I don't remember thinking that these images had anything to do with me. I wasn't traumatized by them or made to feel inadequate about my own feet or body because they had no reference to life as I knew it. I continued to walk up the hill every morning in my sneakers, proud of my strong, big feet. I assumed that my feet would keep growing for a long time.

One afternoon when I was in the fifth grade, I went next door to see Tadashi, a boy who was my best friend. I took off my shoes in the foyer and reached over to straighten them out so they looked neat and orderly—something I was taught to do from an early age as a form of politeness. Tadashi's new sneakers happened to be in the foyer, right next to mine, and I couldn't believe how much bigger they were than mine. Only the year before, our shoes had been the same size. Without my realizing it till that moment, he had grown at least two shoe sizes while my feet had stayed the same. I was sure that there was some mistake—I, too, must have outgrown my shoes without knowing it. For weeks, I kept nagging my mother, claiming that my shoes were pinching my toes. I must have half-believed this myself, but when we went to the shoe store and my feet were measured, they were the same size that they had been. The bigger shoes I insisted on trying almost fell off my feet when I walked around the store. The saleswoman smiled at my mother and said, "So your daughter is eleven now. Maybe her feet have stopped growing." All the way home on the train, I would not speak to my mother even though I knew that what had happened wasn't her fault. The idea that I might have stopped growing—even if it was just my feet and not my height—scared me. There had to be a relationship between how big your feet were and how tall you were; once my feet stopped growing, it would be a matter of time before my height did, too. As we stood side by side on the train, I was still an inch or so shorter than my mother, who wasn't a tall woman at all. If she'd been taller, I was sure, I would have been, too—so I did blame my mother a little. I know now that this was my first almost-unconscious realization of mortality: someday, I would stop growing, and someday after that, I would die. For me, it all happened because of feet.

One thing I could never have imagined even after this vague realization of my mortality was that my mother would choose to die when I was twelve, leaving my brother and me to grow up with our father—who had seldom been home during her life—and the woman he would start living with in a month and marry in a year. From twelve to twenty, I lived with a father whose neglect, I was certain, had caused my mother's unhappiness and death, a brother who quickly lost all memory of our mother, and a stepmother who seemed to take pleasure in making me feel bad about myself every chance she got. She could not make me feel bad about my mind or my performance at school, but my body was an entirely different matter.

My feet grew half a shoe size after the fifth grade. By the time I was in high school, my shoe size was 6½, my height was 5' 3", I weighed a little over a hundred pounds, and I had pretty much stopped growing. Everything about my size was average and therefore "normal" for a Japanese girl my age at that time, and yet my stepmother managed to make me feel like a freak. The part of my body she criticized most was my feet. "Look at how wide and flat your feet are," she would say, clucking her tongue. "It's because your mother let you walk around in those sneakers when you were young. That's how your feet grew so ugly and shapeless. She should have given you hard shoes that shaped your feet better." Glancing down at her own narrow, bony feet, she would shake her head and add, "Your mother made a big mistake. You could have had feet like mine if I'd been around instead of her."

Even though I did not want to have feet like my stepmother's, or wear the spiked high heels she wore which once caused her to drive her car into a neighbor's fence because her heel got stuck underneath the gas pedal, I felt embittered and ashamed every time I took off my shoes in the foyer to enter our house. Now I realize that my stepmother would have bound or cut off my feet, metaphorically or even literally, if she could have: she wanted me helpless, trapped, dependent on her charity. Maybe I sensed it back then, too, but nothing I knew about her maliciousness kept me from feeling bad about myself. I was a teenager, after all.

I think of those eight years as a period during which I hated feet—not just my own, but the whole notion of feet. It was almost as though the whole world outside were conspiring with my stepmother to give me nightmares about feet. Shortly after my mother's death and my stepmother's arrival, almost all of my girlfriends developed a craze for skating. On Saturdays and Sundays, instead of visiting one another's houses or going to record stores or looking at the boutiques downtown, my friends wanted to ride the train for half an hour to a skating rink in a nearby suburb, where we would spend the whole afternoon skating around in circles, listening to the Osmonds or the Partridge Family or other sweet pop music. It didn't take me too long to figure out why. Groups of boys went skating at the same place, also skating in circles, listening to the same music coming from the loudspeakers. Because my mind was always full of sad thoughts about my mother, I couldn't care less about the boys, and I hated skating anyway. All the same, I went with my friends. What choice did I have if I wanted to have friends? I spent a lot of time looking at the chart on the wall, above the rental window. Underneath the writing HOW TO SKATE there were rows of little black feet with arrows and numbers, showing how we should move our feet—toes turned out, the forefoot fanning sideways and then straightened, kick and glide, kick and glide. The more I looked at the chart, the less I could tell which foot was which—right, left, forward, backward. On the ice, my friends were gliding easily; kids of six or seven were twirling on one foot or skating backward, but I was a lousy skater, lucky to go around a few times without falling. I could never keep my ankles straight or stop suddenly by dragging the blade across the ice. After two or three years of this skating ordeal, the whole game was moved indoors to school gyms where, instead of skating, we were supposed to dance at mixers with boys we'd never met before. Again, there was a chart on the wall, showing the box step, the cha-cha, some line-dance moves. The same black feet and the same boys, only a little older and in slow motion. My awkward feet were caught in the mathematical diagram which was worse than geometry.

I resented my mother in those years, not only for choosing to die alone instead of being with me, but also for not having prepared me better for this whole business of growing up. All the stories she told me, especially those involving feet, were bogus. When I was still a little girl, not more than eight or nine, she told me that everyone was destined to fall in love someday. The two people who were supposed to fall in love were connected, from birth, by an invisible red thread tied around their feet. According to her, I, too, had a thread knotted around my smallest toe, and it stretched perhaps all the way around the world to a faraway place, where the other end was knotted around the small toe of the boy I would someday love. I would never have to worry about whether and how I would meet him; over the years, the thread would tug at us and bring us together.

When my mother first told me the story, I didn't think that much about it either way—except late at night, I was afraid of tripping on this thread and falling out of my bed, and I didn't understand how something could be red and invisible at the same time. After my mother's death, though, I hated this story. I wondered if she ever thought she and my father were connected with the invisible red thread, too, and if so, why did their marriage end in her suicide, and what about my stepmother? Did my father have two red threads leading away from his toes, one on each side? I knew it was just a story—a story I hated—and yet I couldn't forget it. I was already cursed or blessed with a writer's mind. In spite of myself, I respected stories.

I began to see that the world was full of stupid stories about feet. My mother had read me the fairy tales of the Brothers Grimm and Hans Christian Andersen. The girl who went dancing in her red shoes, disobeying her mother, would have danced herself to death if it hadn't been for the kind (!) woodcutter who chopped off her feet. The Little Mermaid could exchange her fish's tail for beautiful legs and dancing feet and still die, turning into sea foam at sunrise, all because she could not talk and make her prince understand that she had once saved his life. Cinderella won her prince because she had beautiful small feet while her stepsisters had to slice off their toes to fit into the dainty glass slippers. I also remembered how, during my mother's life, I had played with Barbie dolls—more than their dresses and suits and cars and kitchen sets, I had loved the little plastic shoes that fit like a second skin around the plastic feet with toes all grown into one. In my late teens and into my twenties when I was attending an American college and graduate school far away from home—finally free from my stepmother—I continued to resent the stupid stories and games my mother had allowed me to love as a child. They all had the same message: women were nothing without men and our bodies were decoys in the marriage game. I no longer hated my feet or my body, but I tried hard to cultivate a pure indifference about them. My Buddhist grandmother, I thought, had been right. Detachment was the key to wisdom and happiness.

I became reconciled to my feet at twenty-three, when I took up running again after a five-year layoff. During the high school years when I thought of my feet as awkward and clumsy, I had actually been a dedicated athlete. I ran thousand-meter races and quarter-mile sprints, played on the volleyball and basketball teams, and swam for endurance. My inability to skate had been more an exception than the rule.

When I took up running again in graduate school and started a series of other cross-training activities—weight lifting, swimming—I realized that I wasn't, and perhaps never had been, clumsy. I felt vindicated, and my sense of victory made me appreciate my feet.

The summer I was training for a marathon, my toenails began to turn purple, then black, from the sixty-plus miles I was running every week. I watched their transformation with fascination instead of horror or disgust—the way I used to watch a science project as a child, like the tadpoles slowly growing legs and turning into frogs. It took weeks for the nails to shrivel up and fall off, and when they finally did, there were already new nails underneath— wrinkled and white like the clamshells my mother and I used to collect on the beach near our house. I was thrilled. It was a runner's rite of passage: I had finally run enough to make my toenails fall off.

Especially after I sprained my ankle a few times, I became protective of my feet. I threw away the few moderately heeled shoes I owned and only wore flat pumps, Mary Janes, penny loafers, high-tops, and running shoes. I bought special running socks meant to protect my feet from chafing and blistering. Running or walking, I watched out for cracks in the sidewalks, potholes, loose gravel, and anything that might cause me to turn my ankle. Once again, I loved my feet for being wide, strong, stable. As if to reward me, my feet grew a half size bigger after ten years of running even though by that time, I was in my early thirties. Now, I had plain, powerful size 7 feet, and I loved them.

★  ★  ★

The final transformation of my feet—or my attitude about them—has happened quite recently and it brings me back to the subject of love. Now that I am forty-one, I'm not so scared of the idea that someone might really love me and find me beautiful and cherish every part of my body from my hair down to my feet. When I was younger, I could not bear to hear any man tell me that I was beautiful. It angered me to hear such nonsense. In my thirties, I stopped wearing makeup and started wearing loose-fitting clothes in beautiful colors and fabric—I wanted to play down what was considered to be the beauty of my body and make people notice my impeccable good taste instead. During this period, women loved the way I dressed, and men stopped buying me clothes because my good taste frightened them.

I wasn't shy or self-conscious about my body. In the summers, I wore shorts or T-shirt dresses with flat sandals, and I wasn't embarrassed about people seeing my legs and feet. I live in a small town where very few women my age run. Almost every resident of the town has seen my bare legs at one time or another because my five-to-eight-mile runs every morning take me all over town, on both sides of the river, and if people viewed my legs during their morning commute, that didn't bother me—they were just part of the scenery, no more important than a lamppost. The way I thought about them in my thirties, my legs and feet were purely practical and healthy. I dismissed the idea that they might be attractive or sexy, objects of someone's desire: they were just my legs and feet, something for me to love but not for anyone else. Every time people complimented me on having a nice body, I told them my running regimen.

Sometimes, there is a small gesture that brings on a big change—a magic act that foreshadows or maybe even causes a major transformation although we may perform it unknowingly. I had gotten to my late thirties without having ever fallen in love: though I was married for eleven years and continued to be good friends with my husband after our divorce, what was between us had always been more like a long and comfortable friendship than love. I had concluded that the sort of passionate falling-in-love other people talked about was not for me. I was a granddaughter of a Japanese Buddhist who advocated detachment and resignation, daughter of an unhappy marriage that had originated in love. Love simply wasn't in the cards for me—or so I thought.

As it turned out, I was to fall in love at forty, and I believe that the talisman that forecasted or brought it on was a bottle of nail polish I put on my toenails a few years before this event. The summer of the nail polish, I was working as a volunteer rehabilitator at a local bird sanctuary. When people in my small town found young or injured birds that had fallen from their nests and brought them to the sanctuary, I was one of the volunteers who took the birds home, fed them with a syringe, and let them practice flying and foraging for food in an outdoor cage in my yard until they were strong enough to fly away. I released many of the grown birds in my yard and was curious about where they went—whether they were among the large flocks of house finches and goldfinches that swarmed the feeders hanging outside my kitchen window. My supervisor suggested that I could mark their toenails with a bit of nail polish if I wanted to see—the polish would wear off in a month and never hurt the birds, but this way, if they came back in the meantime, I would know. So I dabbed pink or red polish on the tiny nails of house finches and goldfinches as I held them in my hand, moments before watching them fly up into the air. After releasing a flock of seven finches one afternoon, on a whim, I sat on the picnic bench in my yard and put the same polish—bright red—on my toenails. It was a ritual, I thought, of my solidarity with the birds, a way of wishing them the best on the day of their freedom.

Some of the birds came back to my feeders throughout the summer, though not all, and then the summer was over, there were no more baby birds to be raised, and still, I kept painting my toenails. I liked the way my feet looked with my toes painted red or pink. My stepmother had been completely wrong. My mother had given me beautiful feet. They weren't just strong and functional, but nice to look at—curving smoothly to the widest point, ending with long toes. The nail polish on my toenails—especially in the winter when no one saw my bare feet—became something like a sign of my secret beauty. Later, when I fell in love and my lover noticed my red toenails, I knew that I was sharing my secret beauty with him. That first dab of red nail polish, on the afternoon when I released the seven finches, had forecasted our afternoons together, just as my mother's story of the invisible red thread had been true after all. I had been destined to fall in love. In a way, everything happened because of feet. Falling in love has put a final touch on my lifelong meditations about feet;

something has come to a completion regardless of what happens in the future. Even if we were to fall out of love someday or be separated against our will, my lover and I would walk away, managing two beautiful patterns with our strong feet. Each of us would be anchored to the same ground even as we travel in opposite directions. If the thread that held us together were to break, we would still wear a small remnant of it on our feet, a token of beauty.

The feet are at once the most practical and the most mysterious part of the body. They help us move around on the solid ground, giving us so much range of motion; they allow us to jump up so that at least momentarily, we are airborne. Without our feet, we would be immobile and helpless, though if there is one part of my body that I think of as truly me—representing my consciousness—it is not the feet or even the heart but the head. The head is where I do my thinking, seeing, speaking, hearing, tasting, smelling. It is the most important part of me; I acknowledge this fact every time I put on my cycling helmet. If I were in a small crawl space that was about to collapse, I would of course creep forward, trying to save my head at the cost of possibly sacrificing my feet. But this is exactly what makes feet so mysterious—they are the farthest away from the seat of our mind, our conscious thought. It is such a long trip from the head to the feet. I reenact this mystery every time I go to a shoe store to try on a new pair of shoes. In the corner of the store is the small square mirror meant to reflect only my feet, from ankles down, giving me an exact picture of what a ghost would be lacking. Without fail, my feet in new shoes take my breath away. At once so familiar and mysterious, they anchor me to the ground.

# THE BLESSINGS OF THE BUTT

---

## ROSARIO FERRÉ

### I. GATE OF PLEASURE

I've always had a positive feeling about my butt. It's a part of my body I like, and I am very conscious of it when I walk down the streets of Old San Juan. The rear end is an instant lodestone, a magnet for male eyes in Puerto Rico. If I'm depressed because I've had an argument with my husband, I slip on my tightest *tubo* skirt, climb on my spiked heels and swing down Calle Fortaleza to La Bombonera. There I sit at the counter, my behind sticking out on the red leather stool like a bull's-eye, and order a sweet, squashed, buttered *mallorca* and a *café con leche* loudly, enjoying the amorous looks of neighboring males. As soon as the sweet scent of warm bread and coffee tickles my nostrils, my spirits rise. I don't know why, but I can't feel happy unless I know someone wants to squash my butt like a sweet, buttered *mallorca*. Otherwise, I just seem to mope around and survive.

I suspect it's because of my obsession with the behind that, when I visit the zoo, I head straight for the cage of the apes. I love to watch them. They walk around on their hind legs, using their hands as points of support, so that they grow those large callouses on their knuckles. I feel sorry for them because they got caught in between; they came down from the trees but never stood up completely, coming free of the ground. I look at their skinny rumps, two pink lollypops swinging behind them, half-hidden by thick matts of hair, and I thank God for my generous human derrière.

When our ancestors began walking on two legs instead of four, the buttocks were part of the powerful physical machinery which propelled them forward. Thanks to their large rear ends, they could walk and run faster across the African savannas. They could reach up into the trees to pick fruit or bend down to plant seeds, thus taking the first step towards developing the skills of agriculture. In fact the word *sedentary* comes from the Latin *sedens,* which means to sit. If I can sit on a red leather stool at La Bombonera eating a warm, squashed *mallorca,* it's because one of my ancestor's behind was bigger than the rest and helped him stand upright. That's when he stopped being a hunter and became sedentary, resting comfortably on his butt.

For a female, it's impossible to consider the ass separately from the vagina. Both parts of the body are connected by the perineum, a small triangle of flesh which resembles the South Pole. The perineum sits between two volcanoes, but can feel as cold and distant as Patagonia. There's nothing there except pubic brambles, but it is connected to the vagina, the hallway to that mysterious cavern where life begins and female desire resides. A soft collar of flesh softens the terror of the abyss of birth and pleasure that resides in the vagina's jagged depths. Wise women sit on it as upon a pillowed throne, hiding the triangle over which they reign supreme and to which men render obeisance.

In southern countries buttocks are omnipotent. Sophia Loren and Gina Lollobrigida, for example, both have magnificent behinds—no man can resist them. The ass is mysterious—it's always swishing to its own rhythm under petticoats and skirts and is never even partially revealed like the breasts. In northern countries, however, breasts seem to be more important. The nipples awaken desire and stimulate fantasy, secretly budding beneath silks and gauzes which at the same time hide and expose them to the world. *"Bevete piu latte"* was the paramount masculine fantasy of the sixties, sung by a giant Anita Eckberg in *La Dolce Vita,* Federico Fellini's masterpiece. *"Más pueden mamellas que centellas"* ("Breasts have more power than bolts of lightning"), goes an old Spanish saying.

*"Bendito sea el culo que te parió y las tetas que te amamantaron"* ("Blessed be the butt that birthed you and the tits that nursed you"), I once heard a man yell as I was walking down Seville's Calle de las Sierpes. A feminist today would whirl around and soundly slap the man, proceeding to accuse him of sexual harassment and abuse. But I can't deny I enjoyed it. Maybe that's why I feel guilty every time I hear a man whistle in the street. I know I'm not supposed to like it, but like it anyway. I've felt like that since a trip to Teheran with my husband, when I had to walk three steps behind him and wasn't supposed to lift my eyes from the sidewalk. I never heard a compliment or heard a disrespectful whistle, and also felt frustratingly invisible.

The female behind has been extolled by poets of all ages. In seventeenth-century Spain, for example, Don Francisco de

Quevedo described *las nalgas,* the buns, as "identical twins, born of a unique division." "There is no life as penitent as ours," *las nalgas* complain in his poem "Enigma." "We always go around covered among the crowd, which would consider it indecent if we exhibited our third eye." *"Nuestro tercer ojo"* is a Spanish euphemism for the asshole hidden under our skirts, which affords us another kind of vision, related to primeval instincts.

Luis Palés Matos, Puerto Rico's foremost poet, described how Tembandumba de la Quimbamba, a proud African queen, strode down the streets of the little town of Güayama. In Matos' poem, when Tembandumba shakes her monumental behind, a river of molasses pours from her immense *nalgas* as they press against each other like sugar mill rolls. Tembandumba's ass is an affirmation of Puerto Rican national pride, of its energy and joy.

When I think of sex I immediately think of the word *nalgas.* *Nalgas,* as opposed to buns, is one of those happy, untranslatable words which convey a much richer meaning in one language than in another. They cleave to the rear, move, tremble and swing with a life of their own, while "buns" are static and compact, tempting us with the warmth of freshly baked bread.

Scent is another of the butt's important sexual attributes. It can make a woman powerfully seductive with its marine odor of algae swishing in secret caverns. Odors are often directed towards reproduction, but pleasure also awaits at the end of their labyrinth, crouching like a minotaur that pretends to be tame. It's very different from the breast's sweet odor of milk, of sustenance and warmth which makes us think of childhood. The ass, so near the crotch, can be malevolent, unmanageable, wild. *"Más tira un pendejo de chocha que una locomotora"* goes another

Spanish saying: "A single pubic hair can pull more than a freight train."

Feminist discourse today disapproves of the exposed female backside, the sexual object par excellence, pasted on monster billboards as one sweeps down the beltway at seventy miles an hour. The bikini-clad model advertising Bud or Pabst, for example, strolls down a white sand beach, her blond ponytail swishing over her rump, her hindquarters poised like a pony's, swinging from side to side at the thirsty truck driver blasting past in the July heat. In Puerto Rico, our version of the bikini model in American posters is Iris Chacón, *"la Vedette universal,"* who owns the most famous behind on the island—nearly forty inches wide. Some years ago she did an ad for ESSO Standard Oil on TV. She was filmed leaning on the rear fender of a Chevy, wearing spiked heels and a tiger-skin Spandex coverall, a gasoline hose in her hand. As she daringly inserted the nozzle into the tank she perked up her monumental ass, batted her eyelashes at the consumers and said coyly: *"¡Ponga un tigre en su tanque!"* ("Put a tiger in your tank!") Women as well as men loved it; the ad was a huge success.

Most Puerto Rican women are proud of their gourd-like buttocks, which they like to shake without inhibition at every opportunity. All our popular dances constitute a form of *culo* shaking. Be it *bomba, mambo, plena, salsa, guaracha* or *merengue,* the pivot of our soul is always the butt, where everything is expressed and evil spirits are expelled. We dress to emphasize the wide geography of our *nalgamento* with ruffles, bows and lots of sequins. Women with small bottoms are *chumbas*—figs with sunken cheeks. I've never understood why mainland feminists become so angry when men laud their asses. In Puerto Rico, we feel an immense joy in sharing the beauty of the *culo* with them. When we make love, we hold our partner's ass tenderly, a bun in each hand, the tailbone wiggling happily in between, and let go of everything without guilt or remorse.

## 2. THE BODY'S PURIFIER

I like to picture my body as if it were a canoli: built like a tube or a cylinder of sweet flesh and bones, with a hole on top—my red, lipsticked mouth—and a hole at the bottom—my ass conveniently placed between the buns to keep away insects. Topographically speaking, the esophagus and the intestines, which are respectively connected to the mouth and anus, are really outside my body. They form part of my "outer space," while my heart, lungs and other organs are imbedded in the flesh and occupy my true "inner space." The rear end hides my second mouth, through which I return to the world that which my body has taken from it. The mouth feeds me, the ass purifies me; it expels from my flesh the toxins and undigested fibers that might harm me. Thanks to it I'm a healthy human being.

Defecation is always unheroic and comic. Women are often the brunt of cruel jokes about the butt, for example those of Don Francisco de Quevedo, who wrote to a friend in love with a woman who didn't care for him, trying to cure him of his melancholy: *Just imagine her shitting and you'll stop loving her!* The asshole is the gateway to poisons of all sort which are filtered by the liver and then stored in the gallbladder, but in the romantic, idealized role women have been ascribed through the ages, this very necessary biological activity is taboo. The first time I saw Rodin's muscular *The Thinker,* I burst out laughing. I was sure he was sitting on the toilet, concentrating on a turd. Yet the sculpture is considered a masterpiece. Would the Venus de Milo have been considered a work of art if she had been portrayed in a similar pose?

Shitting and pissing are wasted themes; everybody ignores them. People hardly ever go to the bathroom in Hollywood productions, although in European films there are some exceptions; for example in the Italian film *Sette Bellezze,* Gian Carlo Giannini falls into a trough full of shit as he defecates. There are very few paintings of people shitting, and I've never seen a sculpture depicting this activity. Literature has touched the subject randomly and with a long pole. Cervantes has a hilarious passage where Sancho Panza is so afraid when he hears a clothing mill beating in the dark that he shits in his pants and Don Quijote reproaches him: *"Hueles, Sancho, y no es a rosas"* "You smell, Sancho, and not of roses." In Chaucer's "The Miller's Tale" the hero sticks his rear out the window to shit, and the whole town sees his bare fanny. I don't remember a single scene in classical literature where a woman is described shitting or pissing.

Shitting is one of the few pleasures we have left when we grow old. We may become impotent, give up drinking and eating rich foods, but we go on defecating regularly every day. There's a sensual satisfaction in feeling a large turd slide out; one feels wonderfully relieved afterwards; the body is cleansed and light. This is probably one of the most ignored sensations in literature, yet it should be a rich mine for writers.

Another important activity for the derrière, farting, is more commonly found in writing. Benjamin Franklin, in his *Autobiography*, advises not to keep gases in but to expel them as soon as possible, as retention can be detrimental to your health. As a remedy for their inconvenience in social gatherings he advises chewing on violet breath lozenges, which give farts a pleasant scent. Quevedo wrote a sonnet to *"la voz del ojo, que llamamos pedo, ruiseñor de los putos"* ("The song of the eye, which we call fart, nightingale of sodomites"), probably one of his most scathing.

Farting can be very unromantic, and a fart at the wrong moment can end the most passionate of liaisons. In Laura Esquivel's *Como agua para chocolate*, for example, the heroine avenges herself on her hateful sister, who has married her lover, by preparing all sorts of fancy recipes which make her fart. The young husband soon becomes disenchanted with his wife.

A pesky fart at the right moment can be very effective in getting rid of an unrequited suitor, especially since flatuses tend to follow us around for a while and are not easy to get rid of. On the other hand, the stench of a great fart, of the kind that's truly deadly, a combination of rotten egg, putrid fish and shit, can be as devastating as the atom bomb. It can make even our worst enemy sail instantly away.

Blessed be the female butt, cathedral of *nalgas*, chamber of pleasure, purifier of the flesh, the be-all and end-all, AMEN!

LYNDA BARRY is a writer, cartoonist, and playwright whose work includes *Cruddy, The Freddy Stories,* and *The Good Times Are Killing Me.* Lynda is also the creator of the nationally syndicated cartoon strip *Ernie Pook.*

RON CARLSON's stories have appeared in *Harper's, Esquire, DoubleTake, North American Review,* and elsewhere. He is the author of three short story collections, *The Hotel Eden, Plan B for the Middle Class,* and *The News of the World,* and the novels *Betrayed by F. Scott Fitzgerald* and *Truants.* He teaches creative writing at Arizona State and lives in Scottsdale.

VERONICA CHAMBERS is a culture writer at *Newsweek Magazine.* She is the author of the memoir *Mama's Girl,* as well as three books for younger readers. She lives in Brooklyn and counts the lovely locks of Cassandra Wilson, Kasi Lemmons, and Busta Rhymes among her many hair inspirations. Woo-hah.

LEAH HAGER COHEN is the author of two works of non-fiction—*Train Go Sorry: Inside a Deaf World,* chosen by the American Library Association as one of the best books of 1995, and *Glass, Paper, Beans: Revelations on the Nature and the Value of Ordinary Things,* named one of the ten best books of 1997 by the *Toronto Globe and Mail*—as well as the novel *Heat Lightning.* ROSARIO FERRÉ is the author of *Sweet Diamond Dust, The Youngest Doll, The House on the Lagoon,* and *Eccentric Neighborhoods,* among other works. She is a frequent lecturer in the United States and lives in Puerto Rico. In addition to co-editing and contributing to the collections *Home, Family,* and now *Body,* SHARON SLOAN FIFFER is the author of *Imagining America: Paul Thai's Journey from the Killing Fields of Cambodia to Freedom in the U.S.A.* She is also the co-author with her husband Steve of the book *50 Ways to Help Your Community.* Sharon was also co-executive editor of the literary magazine *Other Voices.*

MICHAEL KNIGHT is a native of Mobile, Alabama. His short fiction has appeared in *The New Yorker, GQ, Paris Review, Story, Playboy,* and *Virginia Quarterly Review,* among other literary journals. He is the recipient of the 1998 New Writing Award from the Fellowship of Southern Writers. Last year, Dutton/Plume published his first novel, *Divining Rod,* and his short story collection, *Dogfight.* He lives with his wife in Charlottesville, Virginia.

NATALIE KUSZ is the author of *Road Song: A Memoir* and the recipient of a Whiting Writers Award, an NEA grant, and other honors. She teaches at Harvard University.

JACKI LYDEN is the author of *Daughter of the Queen of Sheba: A Memoir,* a senior correspondent for National Public Radio, and a regular substitute host for NPR's "Weekend Edition" and "Weekend All Things Considered." An expert on the Middle East, she was part of the award-winning NPR team that covered the Persian Gulf War. Her journalism awards include the 1990 National Mental Health Association Media Award for investigative reporting. When not on the road, Lyden lives in Washington, D.C.

THOMAS LYNCH is the author of three collections of poems: *Skating with Heather Grace, Grimalkin & Other Poems,* and *Still Life in Milford.* His collection of essays, *The Undertaking—Life Studies from the Dismal Trade,* won The American Book Award and was a Finalist for The National Book Award. His work has appeared in *The New Yorker, The New York Times, The Paris Review, Poetry, Harper's, The Irish Times, The Times of London,* and elsewhere. He lives and works in Milford, Michigan, where he is a funeral director, and in West Clare, Ireland, where he keeps an ancestral cottage.

RICHARD McCANN is the author, most recently, of *Ghost Letters,* which received the 1994 Beatrice Hawley Award and the 1993 Capricorn Poetry Award, and the editor (with Michael Klein) of *Things Shaped in Passing: More "Poets for Life" Writing from the AIDS Pandemic.* His work appears in numerous magazines, including *The Atlantic, Esquire,* and *The Nation,* and in such anthologies as *The Penguin Book of Gay Short Stories.* He co-directs the graduate program in creative writing at American University in Washington, D.C.

KYOKO MORI was born in Kobe, Japan, in 1957 and has lived in the American Midwest since 1977. Her publications include two novels *(Shizuko's Daughter* and *One Bird),* a book of poetry *(Fallout),* two books of creative nonfiction *(The Dream of Water: A Memoir* and *Polite Lies: On Being a Woman Caught Between Cultures),* as well as various poems, essays, and short fiction in journals such as *The American Scholar, The Denver Quarterly, The Missouri Review,* and *The Cross-Currents.* After serving as associate professor of English and writer-in-residence at St. Norbert College in De Pere, Wisconsin, Mori has accepted a teaching position at Harvard.

THYLIAS MOSS's most recent books, both published in 1998, are *Tale of a Sky-Blue Dress,* a memoir, and *Last Chance for the Tarzan Holler,* a volume of poetry. The recipient of numerous awards and honors, including a 1996 MacArthur Fellowship, Thylias teaches and lives in Michigan, but could live anywhere so long as she is with her husband and sons.

CHRIS OFFUTT is the author of the short story collections *Out of the Woods* and *Kentucky Straight,* as well as a novel, *The Good Brother,* and a memoir, *The Same River Twice.* His work has received numerous honors, including a Guggenheim Fellowship, a Whiting Award, and an award from the American Academy of Arts and Letters. After ten years of living in the West, Offutt has returned to his home town of Morehead, Kentucky.

FRANCINE PROSE's most recent book is a collection of two novellas entitled *Guided Tours of Hell,* published by Metropolitan Books. She is also the author of ten highly acclaimed novels, including *Hunters and Gatherers, Bigfoot Dreams,* and *Household Saints.* Her short ficton has appeared in *The New Yorker, The Atlantic, GQ,* and *The Paris Review.* The recipient of numerous grants and awards, Prose also teaches at The New School and the Sewanee Writers' Conference.

ESMERALDA SANTIAGO came to the United States from Puerto Rico when she was thirteen. She is the author of *When I Was Puerto Rican, America's Dream,* and *Almost a Woman,* and is the co-editor with Joie Davidow of *Las Christmas: Favorite*

*Latino Authors Share Their Holiday Memories*. She lives in West-chester County, New York, with her husband and two children.

MONA SIMPSON is the author of three novels: *Anywhere But Here, The Lost Father,* and *A Regular Guy.*

JANE SMILEY is the author of many novels, most recently *The All-True Travels of Lidie Newton*. She is presently writing a novel about Thoroughbred horseracing.

# ACKNOWLEDGMENTS

Our heartfelt thanks go to the remarkable group of writers here assembled, our editor Hamilton Cain, our agent Gail Hochman, Jennifer Hershey and Marianne Merola.